Franz Thaler

A

Franz Thaler

Unforgotten

A Memoir of Dachau

Translated by Paul Crichton and Christl Kiener

KIENER PRESS

London, UK, info@kiener-press.com

Title of the German edition: Franz Thaler – Unvergessen
First publishing 1988 by Sturzflüge
Second publishing 1999 by Raetia, Bozen
All rights reserved

16   17   18   19   7   6   5   4

ISBN 978-3-943324-95-2

Typesetting: Kadja Gericke, Arnstorf, Germany
Printed and bound by: CPI Books GmbH, Leck
Cover illustration: Christl Kiener, München
(view from the window of Seeber Farm, Durnholz, South Tyrol)
Cover design: SpieszDesign, Neu-Ulm
Printed in Germany

www.kiener-press.com

Contents

Bearing Witness to the Truth: Franz Thaler's "Unforgotten – A Memoir of Dachau"

In his brief and moving memoir of Dachau Franz Thaler describes his unimaginable suffering at the hands of the Nazis. His father voted in the referendum of 1939 in South Tyrol to let his family remain Italian citizens and not to become citizens of the German Reich. Franz Thaler, then a young man of only nineteen, thought this decision was right and decided not to serve as a soldier in Hitler's army, but to flee to the mountains instead. When his family was threatened with reprisals, he handed himself in, was put on trial and sent to the concentration camp in Dachau. When the American soldiers arrived in Dachau at the end of the war, Thaler and and some of his surviving inmates were not set free, but continued to be held as prisoners. They were transported with others to a camp in France and forced to march during the final stages of the journey. Only then were they finally set free and allowed to return home.

Although there is now a considerable Holocaust literature and a number of well-known memoirs written by survivors of concentration camps, Franz Thaler has made a unique contribution to this literature by writing the only account of a survivor of Dachau which exists in English and has thus helped to give us a fuller picture of the Holocaust. In retrospect the Holocaust is the most important thing to know about the Second World War, and it has had a huge influence on the development of postwar Europe. The principle motivation for the European Union was not economic but political. It was the desire, on the part of, above all, France and Germany, to make it impossible for another war, and another Holocaust, to take place, as the historian, Tony Judt, has very plausibly argued. It is for these reasons, then, that we decided to translate Thaler's book from the original German into English.

Thaler's memoir reminds us that, although the main purpose of the concentration camps, at least after the decision taken at the Wannsee Conference on 20 January, 1942, to implement the Final Solution, was to kill as many Jews as possible, many other people suffered and perished there as well. Thaler himself, who is not Jewish, was sent to Dachau as a political prisoner of the Nazis, and indeed the majority of the inmates of Dachau, the first concentration camp to be set up (on 22 March, 1933, a mere 51 days after Hitler took power), was there because they were considered to be political enemies of the state or criminals. Dachau became a model for the large number of concentration camps which were built subsequently and was a sort of testing ground for increasingly efficient and ruthless methods of control, humiliation, torture and killing of the inmates, and a school for the elite SS guards who were then sent to other camps. These included the members of the Death-Head squads, who were to become the managers of the Final Solution. Subservience was to be achieved by impersonal brutality and methodical cruelty. The guards were encouraged to be creative in developing new ways of humiliating and torturing their inmates. There were also experimental stations in Dachau in which inmates were subjected to a sudden decrease and then increase in air pressure, were made to dive into a cold-water tank and stay there until they lost consciousness, and were deliberately infected with malaria and phlegmon. Not many survived these experiments, which the psychoanalyst, Alexander Mitscherlich, has described in his book "Doctors of Infamy". Far from being kept as a secret chamber of horrors discovered only by American soldiers at the end of the war, it was well-known throughout Bavaria before the war that if you were thought to be a trouble-maker you would be sent to Dachau. Its very notoriety was deliberately used by the Nazis to terrorise and thus control the general population. In this sense it was not a regrettable measure which had to be taken because of the exigencies of war, as some Nazis later claimed in order to exonerate themselves; it was an intrinsic part of the whole Nazi system and was put in place as soon as the Nazis took over power. There were numerous satellite camps attached to Dachau, and Thaler was sent briefly to one of them, in Hersbruck, near Nuremberg. He notes that, despite the appalling conditions in Hersbruck, everyone dreaded being sent back to the even harsher conditions in Dachau, where they were more at the mercy of the SS than in the outer camps.

Primo Levi, who was an inmate in Auschwitz, spoke of "the calm, sober language of the witness", which he himself tried to adopt, and this is also the tone throughout Thaler's book.

Thaler simply relates what he experienced and lets the facts speak for themselves without trying to present them in a dramatic light, and it is this calm and sober voice which makes his narrative all the more powerful. This is not to say that his account is dry and factual: it is not. He describes his emotional reactions to what happened, as these are an intrinsic part of his experience. More than this, his emotions enabled him to see what was happening to him and others, to see injustice and cruelty for what they are, in their proper light. In other words, the emotional response is an essential part of moral perception and moral reasoning, rather than something which distorts these processes. Emotional responses of this kind have cognitive content, they tell us about the world, about moral reality, as the philosopher Miranda Fricker has put it. Thus feeling does not distort his perception and judgment; it informs it.

Another point made by Levi is that he wanted to bear witness *to the truth*. ("The truth" here is shorthand for "the truths" about the Holocaust, as, strictly speaking, there is no such thing as "the truth", i.e. a single truth about the past.) Indeed Levi notes that the survivors of the concentration camps can be divided into two typical categories: those who want to forget and those for whom remembering is a duty. The first group, he explains, are those who ended up in the camps through bad luck, and for whom the experience was like a misfortune or an illness, that is to say traumatic, but devoid of meaning. The second category is composed of "ex-political prisoners, or those who possessed at least a measure of political preparation or religious conviction or a strong moral consciousness". They felt they had a duty to remember because they understand that their experience was not meaningless. Thaler clearly belongs to this second group, and in writing his memoir he becomes part of a distinguished tradition which includes Levi himself, Imre Kertesz, Tadeusz Borowski, Elie Wiesel, and many others, and, before them, Fyodor Dostoevsky and Aleksandr Solzhenitsyn, who described their experiences in a Tsarist labour camp and in Stalin's Gulag respectively. We are inclined to attribute a therapeutic effect to writing about such terrible experiences, but often forget how painful it must have been for many survivors to make themselves remember and re-experience some of that searing pain, even if they felt at the same time that they had to do so.

However some people deny that there is such a thing as an objective truth to bear witness to, and talk about what is true for you, for me or for Thaler, as if Thaler's Memoir told us about what is true only for Thaler, and has no validity as truth for you or me. This topic would merit book-length treatment, but this discussion will be limited to only a couple of points. Relativists about truth complacently claim to be respecting human equality (what each individual regards as true is true for that individual alone, but this is the case for *all* individuals) while at the same time assuming that their conception of relative truth is objectively true. Moreover, they are not really respecting what an individual regards as true at all, but rather refusing to take what that individual regards as true at all seriously as the subject matter of a general discussion, on the grounds that it would have little relevance for anyone else. On the contrary, there *are* many everyday truths, as opposed, say, to complex Freudian interpretations, and language learning would not even get off the ground unless such everyday truths existed. One essential way in which children learn language is through hearing sentences being used in situations in which those sentences are plainly true, as the philosopher, Bernard Williams has argued.

If we accept there is such a thing as the truth about what happened in the Holocaust, it becomes quickly very clear to those who read the literature on this subject that the desire to bear witness to the truth is a powerful motivational factor for survival: people in the camps wanted to make sense of their suffering and one important way of doing so was to live long enough to be able to tell the truth about it to others when they have been liberated. But there is also a deeply tragic aspect to this: the vast majority of those who suffered in the concentration camps did *not* survive and they were deprived, not only of their lives, but also of the opportunity to bear witness to the truth. There are, of course, a few exceptions, and Anne Frank is the most well-known of these. Thus many of those who did survive wanted to tell the world what they had been through. But in doing so they were also telling it, consciously or unconsciously, for the sake of those who had died and who would surely have wanted the world to know.

There is also, especially in films, the strong temptation to give way to sentimentality and stage a "happy end". Both "Schindler's List" and "The Pianist" finish with pictures of the survivors, and not with the mountains of corpses found by the Allied soldiers when they first entered the camps. It is one of the virtues of Thaler's memoir that he resists this temptation, and describes instead, especially in the After-word, how difficult it was to continue living after the war in the small community in the Sarn Valley, with those who had betrayed him to the Nazis and with those who were unable to come to terms with their defeat and continued to keep alive a "good portion of the Hitler mentality".

But why, exactly, is it important to tell the truth about the Holocaust? First, the truth is intrinsically valuable. This can be revealed, as the philosopher, Raimond Gaita, has pointed out, in the ways in which it deepens the lives of those who stand up for the truth. It is "food for the soul" and it is important to many people that they should not live a lie. Thaler is a good example of just such a person. He resisted being drafted into Hitler's army because

"I simply did not agree to fight for the Nazi regime in for-eign countries, and as an Italian citizen I did not feel obliged to do so."

The writing of his memoir and the work he has done to educate young people about the Holocaust, including ac-companying them on trips to Dachau, also show how his commitment to the truth motivated his writing and illuminates his life.

Secondly, the truth should be documented for history. Truth here is instrumentally rather than intrinsically valuable: we want to know who we are, and, in order to be able to do so, we need to know, among other things, where we came from. We also want to try to avoid repeating the mistakes of the past, insofar as our present circumstances are sufficiently similar to those of the past in the relevant respects. Only an accurate record of the basic historical facts can give us this information. And it is only if we know about the unspeakable things which happened in the Holocaust that we can try to ensure that such things never happen again. The killing fields of Cambodia, the massacre of Igbos in the Nigerian-Biafran war of 1967 to 1970, the genocide in Rwanda and Darfur, and the atrocities committed in the Yugoslav wars are a reminder of what a considerable challenge this remains, even if these crimes fall short of the unique horror of what was done in the Holocaust. In the words of the commentary of the "World at War" Thames Television documentary, "Auschwitz is history; racial prejudice still persists".

History is important in another sense too. Tony Judt points out in his book, "Postwar A History of Europe Since 1946", that only after the Germans had appreciated and digested the full horror of their Nazi past – a sixty year cycle of denial, education, debate and consensus – could they begin to live with it. Williams, put it as follows:

"Germans in the last half-century have had a special task which many have pursued with unparalleled determination and honesty, of losing a past without forgetting it."

But "the very enormity of the crime", Judt continues, "renders all memorialization incomplete ... Against this challenge memory itself is helpless". He quotes Yosef Zakhor:

"Only the historian with the austere passion for fact, proof, evidence, which are central to his vocation, can effectively stand guard".

But of course one of the principal sources of history is eyewitness accounts, that is to say memories which have been written down or recorded in some other way. Thaler's memoir is thus an important historical document.

A striking example of the historical significance of Thaler's Memoir is his description of the liberation of the camp and how he and his fellow inmates were treated by the American soldiers. When the inmates noticed that most of the SS guards had disappeared, they started to explore the camp and went into the SS quarters hoping to find something to eat. They came across some shirts discarded by the SS, and, desperate for warm clothes instead of the rags they were wearing, they, rather naively, put on the SS shirts. The American soldiers initially suspected that they were SS men and lined them up against a wall. It was probably only their emaciated and ghostly appearance that led the Americans to have second thoughts and prevented them, at the last moment, from shooting those inmates, who like Thaler himself had put on the shirts innocently. Despite the fact that it must have become obvious by this time that they were *not* SS men, they were held prisoner in barbed-wire compounds with German prisoners-of-war. Late at night some of them managed to escape, but the Americans shot at them, injuring some and killing others. Thaler himself was too weak to even contemplate trying to escape. They were then taken to a camp in France where they were finally set free and allowed to return home. They were forced to march during the final stage of the journey. Thaler could hardly keep up. Someone next to him told him that a straggler had been shot down and had fallen into a ditch. "This was a big blow for me", Thaler remarks, "as I was about to give up anyway".

That the behaviour of American soldiers towards former Dachau inmates was not always impeccable is confirmed by the poet and Nobel laureate, Czeslaw Milosz, in his book "The Captive Mind". In a chapter about his friend, Tadeusz Borowski, (alias Beta, the disappointed lover) the author of "This Way for the Gas, Ladies and Gentlemen", he writes:

"Liberated from Dachau, he became acquainted with the life of refugees in Western Germany. It was like an extension of life in the camp – all the evil forces set loose in men by the years of Hitlerism continued to triumph. The callous policy of the occupying forces towards the millions of recent slaves aroused his anger. Here, then, was the dreamt-of end of the war; again the law of the jungle prevailed; again the strong this time mouthing the slogans of democracy and freedom, trod upon the weak or treated them with cruel indifference."

When Borowski himself was being held by the Americans as a prisoner-of-war in the concentration camp in Allach near Munich (Allach is now a suburb of Munich), where they had sent him from Dachau, he recorded in his diary:

"No doubt the purpose of this whole great war was so that you, friend from Chicago, could cross the salt water, battle your way through all of Germany, and reaching the barbed wire of Allach, share a Camel cigarette with me...And now that they've put you on guard duty, to keep an eye on me, and we no longer talk to one another. And I must look like a prisoner to you, for you search me and call me boy. And your slain comrades say nothing".

The official report of the US Seventh Army on the liberation of Dachau paints a somewhat different picture, one of grateful inmates waving American flags and cheering their liberators. No one would wish to deny that the US forces played a key role in bringing an end to Nazi rule in Europe, that they suffered many casualties and that they faced an unprecedented situation, which must have been very difficult for young soldiers to cope with, when they liberated Dachau. Nonetheless perhaps the time has come for an apology from the US government for their treatment of some of the former Dachau inmates.

After this discussion of some of the implications and the importance of Thaler's determination to bear witness to the truth, I now wish to turn to one pivotal aspect of those experiences, namely his own psychological development during the course of the events he describes in the Memoir. This is not because I think that the evil of the Holocaust can be explained or be made sense of in purely psychological terms, because, as I will explain, this is certainly not possible. But psychology can throw some light on the question of how Thaler managed to survive both Dachau and the terrible journey to France and how he coped with the longer-term consequences of Dachau after he had returned home to the Sarn Valley. Much has been written about what happened, but somewhat less has been said about what it was like to experience these events, how difficult it was for the victims, and indeed for anyone, to try to understand and make any sense of what happened, and especially how hard it was for the victims to cope with the psychological consequences of what they had gone through as they attempted to pick up the threads of their lives again. Thaler's narrative contains many comments which shed light on these topics.

In the referendum of 1939 Thaler's father, Stanislaus, re-sisted the intense Nazi propaganda to opt for citizenship of the German Reich, and voted to let his family remain Italian citizens. His father had already done seven years' military service, four of which were in the First World War, and he saw through the Nazi promises to reconstruct Durnholz and Reinswald somewhere in Germany. Although Thaler was not consulted by his father before this fateful decision was taken, he agreed with it, and decided himself, in May1944, to resist being drafted into the German Wehrmacht, although he knew that if he did so he would have to flee to the mountains.

Looking back after the end of the war he rightly regarded his decision as fully justified. But when his family was threatened with reprisals, he was forced to hand himself over to the Nazis. Initially he was in a state of poignant innocence, the sort of naivety which the Nobel laureate, Imre Kertesz, who was deported to Auschwitz at the age of 14 with other Hungarian Jews, describes with such touching insight in his book "Fatelessness". Thaler thought that he would be made to serve in the army and did not at first realize that he would be put on trial and sent to Dachau. Indeed he did not really have any clear idea of what the implications of being sent to Dachau were. Thus, when he was taken to Dachau by a single armed guard, he made no attempt to escape although he had the opportunity to do so.

However this state of innocence was not to last for long. What followed was the revelation of evil of a vastness which was impossible to grasp. As one former inmate of Auschwitz, Do Pasakowitz or Paskowitz (spelling uncertain), the son of a Hungarian Jewish butcher, put it: "Today I don't believe that there was such a thing. I think it was a dream. But with all that I still see it all today, every detail, as if it happened today" (World at War, Thames Television documentary).

Thaler's first glimpse of what was to come was of a small group of prisoners marching out of the main gate of the camp:

"They were all very thin, their faces were pale, their hair was close-cropped, their striped uniforms were sagging as if they were empty. They wore wooden shoes on their feet. SS men marched to their left and right. A sad sight, especially for me".

What Thaler was about to discover was that normal morality had been turned on its head in the camp. The SS men had been indoctrinated to believe that they were representatives of a "higher Nazi morality" which demanded that they punish the inmates as enemies of the state and that such punishment be meted out mercilessly and unpredictably to engender a state of maximum terror which would make resistance impossible, perhaps even unthinkable. Work was seen principally as just another form of punishment. The lives of the inmates were to be regarded as of no worth. Their human status was reduced to that of objects; they were referred to not by their names, but by their numbers.

That this is a perversion of morality is made clear, among other things, by the fact that the notion of the value and irreplacibility of each individual human being lies at the heart of what we normally take morality to be. Most of us are brought up to believe that individual human beings have intrinsic value and that we should never act in such a way that we treat humanity, whether in ourselves or in others, as a means only but always as an end in itself, as the philosopher, Immanuel Kant, put it. We internalise this belief and come to be partly constituted by it, in other words the belief in the preciousness of each individual becomes part of the fibre of our being. What the Nazis were attempting was something very ambitious, nothing less than the moral reconstitution of the people under their control. Levi rightly noted that the real danger in the camp was not to one's body, but to one's character. Thaler quickly realised this as well, and was all the more astonished when he was on one occasion treated as a human being by, of all people, the Camp Commandant:

"... Then he told me that my sentence had been commuted from ten to two and a half years in the concentration camp. He was pleased, he said, to be able to tell me this. He encouraged me to keep going so that I would one day return to South Tyrol. Tears ran down my face, not so much because of the commutation, but because of the humanity this man let me feel."

In some cases Thaler himself is able to remind us of the humanity of someone who was dehumanized and killed by the SS, by describing him as he was when still alive:

"I could not help thinking of my workmate who had been thrown out of the truck, either dead or at least half-dead. He had been a year younger than me and we had become good friends. He too had suffered greatly from homesickness. I had thought that he was dead after his cruel treatment in the washroom. I would have wished so much for him that he could have seen once again the loved ones for whom he had so yearned. And now, after all the hardships of life in the camp, he had been thrown out of the train like a piece of wood during the transport back to Dachau."

There is a humanity and goodness expressed in these words which shine radiantly in the darkness of the camp. They evoke by way of painful contrast another, now very distant world of peace and family, where each person is regarded as infinitely precious by those close by. As Gaita has noted,

"A tradition, going back to Plato, has taught us that evil can be properly and clearly understood only in the light of the good. In the death camps only that light could illuminate each individual and reveal him or her to be infinitely precious."

The philosopher and novelist, Iris Murdoch, has said that to see the reality of another person is " a work of love, justice and pity ".

Forced to confront an evil which "never has depth...but is only extreme", as the philosopher, Hannah Arendt, expressed it, how did Thaler manage to survive? Part of the reason was because he spent only about five months in the camps. Even so his physical condition became so poor that he might easily have *not* survived. From the psychological perspective there were perhaps three factors which helped him to stay alive: the support of others in the camps, his faith, and the idea of returning home to see his loved ones, but also to bear witness.

Although it was not possible to survive in the camps without a minimal degree of determined self-interest (stealing clothes, basic utensils and food, for instance, was virtually ubiquitous), and although some were themselves corrupted by the prevailing Nazi glorification of force, this does not mean that altruism no longer existed. On the contrary, Thaler describes some outstanding examples of selflessness, for instance Strecker Martl who "was my great guardian and helped me wherever he could". He was older and stronger than Thaler. It turned out that he had the same opinions about Hitler as Thaler and, as an anti-Nazi, had been sent, first to the front with a punishment batallion where he experienced terrible things but survived without injury, and then to Dachau.

"We often prayed together, and not at all secretly or quietly ... We were ridiculed or made fun of by many, but that did not bother us, especially not Martl. If somebody offended him he would rebuke him with a few serious words, so that the latter preferred to move on again. With his thirty-nine years and his serious face he radiated authority so that he was actually rarely pestered. I was pleased about that and felt stronger myself."

Some of those who helped Thaler were also from South Tyrol, such as the two Pichler brothers from the Passeier Valley, but one person was not. An older man emerged from the crowd of prisoners and, seeing Thaler crouched on the floor without any warm clothes, insisted on giving him a thick winter coat, saying he had another one for himself.

"I took the coat gratefully, and was surprised and pleased that somebody had taken pity on me. Without this coat I would definitely not have survived the following days. The man went away from me, disappeared among the prisoners and I never saw him again."

Thaler benefited not only from having a warm coat, but from knowing that there were people who wanted him to live because they saw in him a fellow human being and were moved by their feelings of sympathy to help him.

What also sustained Thaler was his religious faith. He was younger when he was sent to the concentration camp than both Primo Levi and Eli Wiesel, both of whom found it impossible to believe in God. Levi was an atheist and is quoted as saying that there was Auschwitz, and so there cannot be God. Thaler came from a region which has been immersed in Catholicism for centuries. The church of St Nikolaus in Durnholz, very near where Thaler lives, was built in the 13th century and contains some famous Higher Gothic frescoes. There is never a single moment in the Memoir when he expresses the slightest doubt about his faith, despite all the horrific things he experienced in Dachau. This seems to me rather remarkable in itself. But it is not so much that evil, and especially the evil of the concentration camps, is beyond our comprehension because we lack the cognitive capacity to understand it. It is rather that evil is simply mysterious, full stop, and so there is no possible explanation which religion, science or metaphysics could ever offer. Linked to his unbroken faith was his hope of returning home to his family and friends. Throughout his time in the camp he prayed:

"I prayed again and again and particularly when the situation seemed to be desperate I gained new hope from prayer".

But it is not only evil which is intrinsically mysterious. It is goodness as well. The particular kind of goodness I have in mind is the complete absence of bitterness in Thaler's Memoir, and in the man himself. When I asked Thaler about this, he repeated what he had written in his book, namely that he had forgiven but not forgotten. He was referring to the individual people in the Sarn Valley who betrayed him to the Nazis. The Sarn Valley is quite a small place where everyone knows everyone else, and it must have been extremely difficult for Thaler, when he came home in 1945, to live again in such close proximity to his betrayers. Some of them became his customers and bought articles of quill embroidery which he had made for them. Thaler notes:

"I was pleased to be needed by them now, although they would have preferred to 'eradicate' me at that time. If the dear Lord is merciful to them as well, which I would wish for them, then everything is alright."

It is easier to forgive someone if they show remorse, as Thaler rightly observes. But he also writes:

"I have never heard anyone say he should not have done or said something – neither the simplest ,voter for Germany' who mocked us as , 'Walsche' (i.e. Italians) nor the big village Nazis who unjustly sent me and others to the concentration camp or to prison or to the front."

So forgiveness could not have been easy under these circumstances, and seems almost as mysterious as the evil itself. Some light may be shed on this by Nelson Mandela. In a book of essays on the Truth and Reconciliation Commission in South Africa, called "Commissioning the Past", Mandela writes:

"I am often asked how it is that I emerged without bitterness after so long a time in prison...Millions of south Africans spent an even longer time in the prison of apartheid...in such circumstances personal bitterness is irrelevant...Instead we must insist with quiet resolve on a firm policy of undoing the continuing effects of the past".

This view, I think, would probably be shared by Thaler, who himself insisted on just such "a firm policy of undoing the continuing effects of the past" by doing educational work with young people, which included accompanying them on trips to Dachau.

But Thaler is at the same time characteristically clear-sighted and forthright about the excuses and obvious lies of some of the people he met:

"Whenever somebody asked me about my experiences in Dachau I was often interrupted in my description by those who had a different opinion and who then said that it was finally time to stop talking about these old matters and to forgive and forget. I could only always say the same thing to them: , 'You have no idea about everything there is to be forgotten and forgiven'. People cannot imagine the physical and mental torture in the concentration camps unless they have experienced it themselves. I think that we who were persecuted by the Nazis were generous in our forgiving."

Some people who were known to have been Nazi informants and collaborators repeatedly denied that they had been involved and had betrayed anyone. Others used "the great excuse" that they had to do it, otherwise they would have had to join up immediately. Thaler's response is incisive: "So they stayed at home at the expense of others whom they unscrupulously imprisoned". In retrospect, Thaler may well have thought, they should have simply refused to send other people to the camps, and thus sometimes to their death, whatever the consequences.

With regard to Thaler's remark about not forgetting, what happened in the immediate postwar years can best be described as a "collective amnesia". Thaler wanted therefore to connect people with the truth. In "The Voice of Memory" Levi mentions the frequent nightmare of many concentration camp inmates of escaping and "telling their story and not being listened to". This is a strong indication, I think, that the truth is intrinsically valuable, quite regardless of the consequences of its becoming well-known. And it is in this sense that Thaler's powerful memoir bears witness not only to the events he experienced, but to the value of truth itself.

Paul Crichton,
London 2013

Franz Thaler

Unforgotten

A Memoir of Dachau

First Signs

In May 1985 I visited the former concentration camp of Dachau, in which exactly forty years ago, on the 29th of April, the gate to freedom had been opened for me and my friends. In the camp, I went straight to the museum in which various documents and photographs from the years 1933 to 1945 can be seen. At the sight of some of the photographs tears came once again to my eyes. Along with me there were many visitors from very many different countries. These included a particularly large number of young people. On their faces one could read horror. In the large room it was almost completely silent. You could hear only a low murmur.

In the afternoon I had a look at the two remaining barracks, the square where so many had been hanged, the so-called ditch of blood where so many lost their lives as a result by being shot in the nape of neck, and finally the crematorium, in which thousands who were emaciated, just skin and bone, who had been beaten to death, shot or starved "went through the chimney" of the furnaces, as they said in Dachau. The gas chambers can still be seen, but they were never put into operation. The death candidates in Dachau were sent to other camps. Finally I visited the three chapels of atonement which were built later: the Protestant, the Jewish, and, in the middle, the Catholic chapel, the "Chapel of the

Agony of Christ". The Carmelite monastery is situated behind these, and in its church I prayed for my dead comrades.

During the visit I thought a great deal about the days and years which had gone by.

The first signs of my journey to Dachau were already evident in 1939. In June of that same year Nazi Germany and Faschist Italy had started the resettlement of the South Tyrolians. They gave us the so-called "Option". People were forced to decide either to opt for German citizenship with the explicit obligation to migrate to the Great German Reich or to keep their Italian citizenship, but with the threat that they would not be allowed to claim any minority rights whatsoever. Those who made no declaration at all remained Italian citizens. The notorious head of the SS and the Gestapo, Heinrich Himmler, was given the task of implementing the agreement. But I knew and understood nothing at all about all of that, being a fifteen-year-old farmer's boy. I remember only that people were terribly frightened when they heard about this agreement. Most of them could not believe it. It just could not be true.

This was the mood in July, and also at the beginning of August, in the Sarn Valley and indeed in the whole of South Tyrol as well. We heard more and more frequently about secret gatherings and meetings. Groups of Bavarian singers came into the valley. They were well received by the Untereinswald group. The singers soon appeared in Durnholz as well, where I lived. They sang German songs up in the choir. As their arrival had been announced in advance, many people came along. The priest on one occasion made

31

a pointed remark because the churchgoers kept looking up to the choir. He said, "Are those up there holier than those at the altar?" I think he already knew what was in store for us. In September and October people talked more and more about voting, and that, of course, one would have to vote "German". Waves of fierce propaganda swept through the valley. It was initiated by the "Völkischer Kampfring Südtirol" (VKS)*, a Nazi-orientated alliance which had its people positioned everywhere in the country. But what did I know about the VKS at that time? Even it was originally strongly in favour of remaining Italian. After several discussions with Himmler it changed its position completely. Now it wanted a hundred-percent result in favour of German citizenship and of bringing about migration in order to create a very favourable impression in Berlin.

Some preparatory work to achieve this result had already been done in school. I remember well that we school boys often said: "Our Father, who art in Heaven, Mussolini on the dung heap, Schuschnigg next to him and three cheers for Hitler."

The Option, the "vote", created a deep division in the people. Many families in the Sarn Valley were also torn apart. Some of them decided to leave things as they were, others were very keen to "vote German". The propaganda efforts to convince people to leave things as they were were quite weak. But there were still enough people who stuck to the resolution they had made in June to be shot rather than to vote for migration.

---

* Translators' footnote: VKS = the ring of the people's fighters of South Tyrol

I lived at that time, not with my family in Reinswald, but with my uncle in Durnholz. There I was treated as a member of the family.

In the latter part of October I heard that a certain Canon Gamper held a meeting at Hofmann's in Reinswald, in which he spoke out against the option and strongly in favour of leaving things as they were. The young farmer I was staying with at that time, as well as the neighbour's two daughters and farmhand, had also gone to this meeting. They came home in the early morning quite agitated and told us at breakfast about everything they had heard. Gamper, they said, threw light on the true nature of National Socialism and on the persecution of church and religion. Hitler had already driven the German people to war and no one knew how this would end. The people should stick above all to their native land. They would never get another one like it. The promises of the Nazi propagandists, that they would reconstruct in Germany a Durnholz and a Reinswald exactly the same as in the Sarn Valley, were complete nonsense. The stories about every migrant getting the same house and the same farm were obviously lies.

At that time of course I had no idea who this Canon Gamper was. It was only after I returned home that I discovered that he was the intellectual leader of the resistance against faschism and National Socialism. After the invasion of Italy by the Germans in September 1943, Gamper was able to make a narrow escape from the Gestapo bloodhounds and flee to Florence.

The young farmer also said that during the meeting a Nazi propagandist had run into the room and shouted: "What he is saying is a pack of lies. Don't believe him!" The man was even about to attack him, but some men grabbed hold of him and dragged him out through the door.

A few days later we went to the neigbours in the evening to play cards. There we met a travelling salesman who was staying there overnight and who had witnessed everything that had happened at the meeting in Hofmann's. Among other things he told us what had happened after Gamper's speech. Gamper had said that those in the audience who wanted to remain Italian citizens would have the opportunity to vote right away because he had the necessary forms with him. At that the point the old watchmaker spoke up and signed. He addressed his brother and said: "Stanis, you are going to sign as well, aren't you?" And Stanis went up as well and signed for himself, his wife and for his six underage children.

When the travelling salesman said that my blood ran cold. Everyone present stared at me and I only looked at the table-top because Stanis was my father and the watchmaker my uncle. Somebody said to me: "Your father has voted 'walsch'*. You are a 'Walscher' now." I did not know what to say and I already felt almost like an outcast. Then the farmer's wife said, in order to console me: "We'll simply pack Franz in a chest and smuggle him into Germany." Everybody laughed, I was the only one who did not feel like laughing. We went home.

---

* Translators' footnote: walsch = Italian

For me this was the first blow I was dealt by the Nazis.

On the farm not much was said about this matter. The farmer was in favour of staying Italian, his siblings were in favour of migrating.

The following Sunday I went to my parents in Reinswald. I was curious to hear what they had to tell me. They explained to me why they had voted "walsch", why they had followed Michael Gamper's advice and why they did not want to give up their native land of their own free will. They reminded me that they had lost their home once before because of hard times. Now they had only just managed to built a very modest little house for themselves.

My father had done seven years' military service, three of which were active and four were in the war. He had been out in the world long enough, and did not want to leave home for a second time. My parents said: "Don't mind if they call you the 'Walscher'. The rumour that we would be transported to Sicily was only made up by the Germans because they begrudge our staying here." My parents convinced me and I thought their decision was right. Of course I could not tell my fellow voters in Durnholz.

So the first weeks in December 1939 went by. The propaganda and the enthusiasm for "voting German" grew steadily.

The "voting day" was supposed to be a celebration. The people of Durnholz were supposed to walk in a single group, accompanied by the band, to the town council in Sarnthein in order to vote. This was the plan and the wishes of the great and the good in Durnholz. And they achieved their aim to a large extent. In Durnholz there were only three familiies of whom it was known that they had decided to stay Italian. Some people kept it secret because they did not want to be exposed to ridicule and contempt. The "Walschen" were ridiculed by everyone and even in church people laughed and whispered behind their backs. On the church square and on the way to church they were greeted with a vociferous "Buon giorno". They could not show their faces in some public houses. In others the chair on which a "Walscher" had been sitting was wiped clean.

After the option in 1939 a German teacher came to Durnholz. Previously there had been only Italian teachers who taught Italian exclusively. The new teacher was now supposed to teach adolescents the German language.

One Sunday afternoon the children and adolescents assembled in the school. I went there as well without suspecting anything. The new teacher wrote down all the names. When it was my turn I of course wanted to tell him my name. But others anticipated me and shouted: "But he is a Walscher." Everybody laughed. The teacher looked at me for a moment and said I should go home, he wanted to teach only Germans. I sat there stunned, then I got up and walked in a daze out through the door. I was very, very sad.

It went on like this for a few years.

In the years 1942–1943 quite a lot of people were called up for military service in the German Wehrmacht. And it did not take long for the first reports of soldiers killed in action to arrive. Now those who had previously shouted "Heil

Hitler" railed against this same Hitler more and more frequently. The great enthusiasm for Hitler quickly faded away. People were already saying that this same Hitler could lose the war.

Escape to the Mountains

And so it continued up to September 1943. After the Italian capitulation the German troops occupied most of Italy, and of course South Tyrol as well. The provinces of Bolzano, Trentino and Belluno were joined together to form an "operational zone 'Foothills of the Alps' ". Franz Hofer, the Nazi Gauleiter of Innsbruck, was appointed as the highest-ranking commissar for this area. The Nazi fat cats now gained the upper hand again. Those who had remained Italian citizens were prey to every possible harassment. Their leaders were hunted down like criminals. They took the radios and the hunting guns from all those who had remained Italian. (My friend Friedl Volgger published a list of the Nazi victims. From September 1943 to the end of the war in May 1945 twenty South Tyrolians were executed, a hundred and forty got to know life in prison and a hundred and sixty-six were taken to concentration camps.) The most senior commissar set up police regiments, in which those who stayed behind were also enlisted, although they were Italian citizens. I know today that the enlistment in German military units of those who had remained Italian citizens represented a gross infringement of international law.

In March 1944 I was called up with others who had remained Italian, and who were aged between 16 and 50.

I was declared fit and knew that I had to join up soon. At the end of May I received my orders to join the army and I was told to report on the first of June at the police station in Schlanders. I desperately tried to find a way out, as I had already heard about too many of the atrocities which the Hitler regime had perpetrated. And so I decided to follow the advice of some of my friends and to flee to the mountains. They promised to supply me with food. I was allowed to collect milk at night from one of them.

The day I had to join up arrived. I packed my suitcase. I did not want anybody to see me doing this because I packed only my rucksack and a little something to eat. In the morning I went to Sarnthein. A Nazi spy was already waiting there to help me find the right way to Bolzano. He accompanied me and explained to me in Bolzano exactly where and when the train to Schlanders would leave. I finally managed to get rid of him. I hid my suitcase at the Rösslwirt in the Bindergasse and went with my rucksack to the station. I had already inquired about when the train would leave for the Brenner Pass. I went as far as Freienfeld, the stop before Sterzing, and walked from there to Maria Trens where I prayed for a happy future. Later I went back by train to Vahrn near Brixen and walked back in the direction of my home, along the Schalderer Weg. That is where I experienced my first mishap.

In the forest, on a narrow bend with no way of escape, I came across a well-known Nazi from my village. We exchanged greetings and continued walking. He went downhill and I went uphill. What on earth should I do now? I knew he would betray me when the military reported that

I had not arrived in Schlanders. I would have to think of something. I had the idea of going back home for an indefinite period. So I returned to the farm where I had been before and told them what had happened to me. I worked for another week on the farm. On a Saturday I told the people that I had received a letter and that I had to leave again on Monday, because it would have been too dangerous for the farmers to let me stay any longer.

That Monday, at three o'clock in the morning, I went up the mountain with the necessary food, a pan, a bowl and a spoon in my rucksack. I wanted to wait there until the end of the war. The first day seemed to me to be infinitely long. I thought hard about everything I would have to give up and about what dangers I would be exposing myself to. I must not let anyone see me. Nobody must know that I had not joined up, apart from the few friends whom I had already told about it. I could go to certain people only at night to collect some food. The meals were very modest. It was very seldom that I had warm food because I had to be very careful about lighting a fire. The smoke should not reveal my hiding place. I cooked mostly dumplings, which turned out to be rather hard because a lot of the ingredients were missing. If something was left over I ate it the following day. Later in summer, when the forest fruits were ripening, I stewed some fruit or made polenta with blueberries or raspberries. My brother Flor, who was working on the other side of the mountain as a herdsman, usually supplied me with butter and cheese. Another "supplier" was my cousin, Luis (Alois Brugger from the Bachmann farm), and there were many others. I must not forget to mention a friend from the Eisack Valley, Felix Oberrauch (Latzfons) who was employed at that time as a herdsman at the mountain pasture where I was staying. He gave me moral and practical support. I often had to change the place where I was staying. It would have been too dangerous to keep sleeping in the same place. For this reason I used various hay sheds and the deserted mountain pine factory. Month after month went by. I got used to many things.

Once, when I was strolling through the forest, I saw to my horror two men standing behind a tree. I immediately tried to make myself scarce. But one of them shouted after me: "Stop, Franz, you don't need to be frightened of us." I recognized the voice. It was "Krotzer" Luis from Villanders, whom I had got to know quite a few years before when he was working in the mountain pine factory, where I had now been staying quite often in the last few weeks. I went up to the two of them a little hesitantly. Luis assured me that I need not be afraid of his companion, because he was a friend. To be on the safe side I decided not to trust them completely, and stayed at a distance of two or three meters. I asked them what they were doing here. They replied that they were on patrol duty at the Villanderer Alm*. Because nothing at all was going on up there, they just came here over the ridge, across the Durnholz mountains.

To combat my boredom I had thought up a suitable activity which required almost no tools and no space. I engraved cigarette lighters and tobacco tins, matchboxes and

---

* Translators' footnote: Alm = mountain pasture

various other things. Often I worked on top of a high spruce. I settled high up on a big branch, where nobody could see me; I screwed the manually operated grindstone on to the next branch. So I had a pleasant view, and I was able to earn some money for food with this work.

Once I helped a farmer with the hay, at a spot where no footpath went by. I positioned myself on the hay cart and kept watching closely to see if there was anybody around. Soon after work started, I saw a man approaching us from a distance of about a hundred and fifty metres. I mentioned this to my fellow workers and walked away swiftly in the direction of the forest. At that time it was well-known that I was hiding up on the mountain. The man who had come was a Nazi spy. I recognized him right away. He asked my fellow workers who the person was who was with them. As they were reluctant to answer immediately, he remarked that he had already recognized me. He also urged them to be more cautious. It was strictly forbidden to work with people like me.

This could have had serious consequences for the farmers. I did not go to their place any more. But I made wooden shoes for the farmer's wife; in return she gave me food.

(After my return I met the man in question again. We greeted each other. He behaved rather sanctimoniously, and assured me that I would not have had to leave the hay making that day, that he had not been one of them, and that he would certainly not have betrayed me. But that was the way they all behaved after the war. Nobody wanted to have had anything to do with the Hitler regime. I said nothing and went on my way.)

There was one worry which never left me: I could not become seriously ill. I certainly could not go and see the doctor, because the doctors that I knew were on the side of the Nazis. But one day it became nevertheless necessary for me to risk seeing a doctor.

One Saturday there was a big thunderstorm and it destroyed the roof of the hay shed where I had made my quarters. During the night, in rain and hail, I had to mend the roof, at least provisionally. The following day, on Sunday, the Feast of Guardian Angels, I had to finish the repair of the roof so that nobody else would come to do it. Because I was soaked to the skin I caught a cold and suffered from terrible toothache which would not stop. I went to my friend Lex to get his advice.

He had always been a wily fox and immediately found a solution for me. He said: "I will go with you to Brixen tomorrow to a dentist called Müller, whom I know well. Nobody knows you there and everything will soon be alright again." And that is what happened. When we walked through Brixen, I did not feel very comfortable. We came across quite a lot of policemen and military people. To my horror we were even stopped by a guard. But fortunately for me he was a friend of my companion. He only wanted to chat a little with him. The dentist extracted my tooth and fixed me up with another one. Without further incident I returned again to the mountains.

At the beginning of August the hay was taken in. I was lying in a shed and looking outside through a gap in the wall. I saw an old man, Seeber Luisl, close by, coming up to the shed. It would have been dangerous to be seen by him. He would certainly have told the people in the village. I squeezed up close to the wall in the shed, between the hay and the kitchen. It was high enough but did not go up to the roof. People had the habit of looking into the shed when they walked past, to see how much hay was in it. Luisl went into the kitchen and mumbled to himself for a while. Because he was not tall und could not see behind the wall, he took a stick and wanted to use it to measure the level of the hay that was stored there. In doing so he poked around at me for a time. The situation was so funny that I nearly burst out laughing.

On another occasion, when I was lying again on the hay, I saw Eben-Sepp (Josef Hochkofler, Bachmannebner, born 1891) coming along. I was not in the least afraid of him. He had been through the First World War and was, for some years, a prisoner-of-war of the Russians. His son Sepp was my best friend at school. He came into the kitchen and was very surprised, when he looked over the wall at the hay, to see me lying there. "Oh, it's you. This really must be a hard life. Hopefully it doesn't last long until the war is over." I asked about his son Sepp who had been called up in spring when he was seventeen. We chatted for a while; then he left again. At the beginning of September a brother of mine was supposed to join up. My brother fled with his friend. But the two of them had been a bit careless. When they stopped by at a relative's house one evening, they were seen by a Nazi spy who reported it to the police right away. Before the two of them could suspect what was happening, the house was surrounded by policemen and Nazi people, a sort of South Tyrolian auxillary police force. The fugitives turned off the light and rushed out through the front door into the open, one to the right, one to the left. My brother's friend was grabbed by his rucksack by a policeman when he was jumping over the fence, and the policeman overpowered him. But the would-be prisoner was very agile and was able to escape after all.

Why I turned myself in

For me things were now becoming more and more difficult. The police increased their efforts to capture fugitives. Soon it was made known that the whole families of the draft resisters would be arrested unless the latter turned themselves in.

And in fact the Nazis had introduced a law to arrest whole families, as I was told on my return. The highest-ranking commissar, Gauleiter Franz Hofer, had passed a decree as early as 6th of January 1944, according to which all who did not obey the order to join the army were to be sentenced to death, or, in less serious cases, to be given ten years' imprisonment. The family members of the fugitives, namely the wife, the parents, children above the age of eighteen and siblings living in the same household were arrested. The relatives were sent to prisons and labour camps. In the Passeier and Ahrn valleys dozens of families suffered this fate. But as I mentioned before, I heard about this only when everything was over.

And this is how it came about that my father started looking for me. And he found me with the help of my younger brother. With tears in his eyes he asked me to turn myself in. Nothing would happen to those who turned themselves in, so it was said. I did not trust the promises of the Nazis at all. But I no longer had a choice. In order to save my parents from imprisonment I promised my father to come home that very evening.

That was the end of my life as a fugitive. It had not been a pleasant life. Often I felt like a wild animal that startles and flees at the slightest noise. But I would not have thought that I would end up turning myself in to the Nazis voluntarily. This would not have happened if my parents had not been threatened with arrest.

And so I went home that evening. The responsible officer came right away. He spoke very highly of me because I had turned myself in. He promised me and my parents to make sure that nothing would happen to me because I had fled.

The Policeman in Schlanders

The following day, on the 23rd of September 1944 I went to Bolzano and reported there as the responsible officer had explained to me. I had the impression that everything had been already prepared. There were only a few questions that they asked me. Then I received my conscription orders and was told to go to the police in Schlanders. There I had to report to the sergeant major of the 10th company. The following day I had to march out with the company. I met many acquaintances from home. They were surprised to see that I had only just arrived. Some said that this was not fair. But I did not want to say much about my past, and I particularly wanted to keep it secret from the officers. I was afraid my cover would be blown. And then things might go wrong.

And so a week went by. Everything seemed to be just fine. I soon found good friends who helped me wherever they could. I had to catch up on three weeks of training. For me this was a tremendous change from my very solitary life to the very active life of a soldier. I felt normal again because I was once again among people. In my heart I still felt a certain fear that I could still face disaster. People in the barracks said that things had gone very badly for other deserters.

The training was finished. We were told that all of us could have a short holiday before we would be deployed. All the others, one by one, went on holiday. I hoped to do so as well. I would have had a last chance to flee because it was becoming clearer and clearer to me that I would be arrested at some point.

My inner fears did not deceive me, as it turned out. On the morning of the 22nd of November the 10th company was told to go to other barracks to be inoculated. We marched there as a company and were led into the inoculation room. We were summoned in alphabetical order. Suddenly someone shouted out my name from the entrance door. I was alarmed and knew: this is it. I said to myself: "God have mercy on me." At the door a guard screamed at me with a fairly harsh facial expression and harsh words that I should hurry up and follow him. We went to the major. We entered; I went first, the guard immediately behind me. I was ready for anything.

The major was already waiting for us. In spite of my trembling knees I tried to salute smartly. The guard announced me. The major asked me whether I was Franz Thaler from the borough of Sarn Valley, born on the 6th of March 1925. I answered: "That's correct, major." Then he read me a document which contained the following: "You were summoned on the 6th of June to the police station in Schlanders and did not obey this summons. You roamed around the mountains" etc. etc. Finally he asked me whether this was correct. I answered: "Yes, it is, major." He told me that I would be taken to Bolzano the following day and stand trial before a military court. With that I was dismissed.

The guard brought me back to the barracks where I had to pack my things. I also had to remove my shoe-laces, my braces and my belt. But I had to laugh at this. The trousers had been so loose, so very loose that I always needed to hold them up with one hand. While I was fumbling around with my trousers my roommates returned from their inoculation. Of course they looked very surprised when they saw me standing like that with the guard behind me with his pistol at the ready. They looked at me with pity. In the meantime the other companies had reported and immediately found out what had happened to me. Several comrades came to the door, and I smiled at them. It was a silent farewell from my comrades and my life in freedom.

Before the Military Court

Gradually I had recovered from the initial shock and accepted my fate. The guard took me to the prison where the head of the prison received me. He walked in front of us through a long corridor which became darker and darker right up to the door of the last cell. He rattled the keys and unlocked the door. In the semi-dark room I saw, fairly high up, a small barred window. Then somebody switched the light on. It did not become much brighter, but bright enough for me to be able to see who was in the cell. There were four men standing to attention in the room. This was an order which was to be strictly followed if somebody unlocked the door. One of the men, Alois Darocca, born in 1904, an older man, looked so confused and desperate that I too became frightened. I entered the room and the iron door snapped shut behind me. I saw a broad wooden bunk with a few blankets on top of it. A young lad invited me to sit next to him. He was Anton Königsrainer from St. Leonhard in Passeier (born in 1921). When the guard had disappeared we sat down on the bunks. Now it was time for questions and answers.

The older man reported that he had deserted and was later caught by the police. He had been sentenced to death. Whenever the door opened he thought they were coming to take him to be shot. Another man, Franz Hauser from

St. Leonhard in Passeier, said that he had enlisted, but had fled after a few days. As they had threatened to lock up his parents, he turned himself in and was then sentenced to twelve years in the concentration camp in Dachau.

They gave the third man, Anton Königsrainer, a sentence of fifteen years in Dachau for the same offence. The fourth man had been there only a few days. One can imagine that the atmosphere in the cell was rather sombre.

The black and grey walls, several metres thick, helped to make it almost impossible for us to even smile. I thought about what sentence I might expect the following day. Things did not look good for me. I had been on the run for almost four months and one of my brothers was still on the run. This was certainly another disadvantage for me. That night I slept little: the day had been too unsettling. It was only in the early morning that I finally fell asleep.

At seven o'clock we heard the head of the prison come with the keys. He unlocked the door and a guard who had been in my company stood beside him. I had to get ready to leave. The guard said to me that I should follow his orders strictly. We went to the station. I went ahead, he immediately behind me with a pistol in his hand. I was not allowed to look to the left or to the right. At the station we immediately got on to the train and I was allowed to sit down. The passengers looked at me full of pity. The guard remained standing right beside me. He was obviously extremely frightened that I might take off. After some time I had to go and relieve myself. First he did not want to let me go. But in the end he gave me permission. But he walked right behind me. I was not even allowed to lock the toilet door.

It took us a very long time to get to Bolzano. On the way there was an air-raid alarm; the train had to stop for some time. It was only at about eleven o'clock that we arrived in Bolzano. There we walked to a large building. We went in and walked along a long corridor to a door where a man was standing guard. Of all people it was an acquaintance of mine from the Eisack Valley. He asked us what we were doing there. The guard replied that he had to take me to a court hearing. My acquaintance pointed to the door through which we were supposed to enter. He smiled at me and said that things would not be so bad.

There was a long table in the room behind which eight to ten SS men with sneering expressions on their faces were sitting. The guard announced me. Now I knew that I was doomed. At the age of nineteen, I was appearing before a military court merely because, as an Italian citizen, I did not want to be forced to join the German army.

One of the men started to question me. I answered. He read me out the minutes. After I had confirmed their accuracy, he ordered another man to read out the article of the military penal code which applied to me. I prayed silently, but was ready for anything. The article which applied to me stated: "Whoever resists military service will be sentenced to death." There was a short silence. The men grinned at me contemptuously. I had the impression that they expected me to faint. But I only smiled at them. How I still summoned the strength to smile surprises me even today. Probably the whole host of angels whom I had just implored was standing at my side.

One of the SS men took a sheet of paper from the table and read out: "Because the accused is still a minor and surrendered of his own free will, he will not be sentenced to death, but to ten years in Dachau, with a suspension of his sentence followed by military service on the front." He then looked at me and asked if I had anything more to say. I said I did not. I was very surprised about the sudden change in the verdict. I did not know what ten years' concentration camp in Dachau would involve. Fortunately I had no idea what Dachau meant.

After the announcement of the verdict I was dismissed and returned to Schlanders. The grey, cold prison awaited me there. The fellow prisoners had been waiting for me with fearful curiosity. When the heavy prison door fell to behind me, I told them what had happened to me. A death sentence would have been terrible, not only for me and my relatives. It would also certainly have had consequences for the Nazis in my village. They were already receiving threats from the partisans.

That evening I was very tired because the day before with the arrest, followed by an almost sleepless night and a very upsetting day, had made me feel exhausted. The only thing I wanted was to sleep, nothing but to sleep.

The following day normal prison life began. The routine was roughly as follows: at half-past six we crawled, one after another, out from under the blankets. There was a rubbish bin in one corner which served as a toilet. That, of course, was not very pleasant. In addition a cloud of gas escaped from the bucket whenever the lid was lifted. That is why the air in the cell was always foul. In the other corner there was a trestle with a bowl and a jug of water. The jug was so small that there was not enough clean water in it for all of us. We all had to wash our faces and eyes with the same water. That was all the water there was. We were then given coffee. A soldier always had to bring us our meal from the military kitchen. We received exactly the same amount as the soldiers. The meals were usually cold by the time we got them.

After breakfast we tidied up the cell as best as we could. We shook the blankets, which were sticky and full of lice and fleas. The straw on the bunks was ground to powder. It had probably not been changed for months. We then sat down on the bunks and started to pray. From ten to eleven o'clock we were allowed to go out into the prison yard where we emptied the rubbish bin and could fetch water for the following day. The yard was surrounded by a high wall; a guard was always standing on a balcony. It was in the yard that we met the four clergymen who were imprisoned in a cell next to ours.

At twelve o'clock they brought us food and afterwards we crept back under the blankets for a while. Later we discussed things for some time. Once more we started praying. Toni Königsrainer was always the one who started and led the prayers. Three times a week we were allowed to attend mass in the clergymen's cell and also to receive communion. The clergymen enjoyed a little more freedom. They could walk around in the corridor and also passed by the door of our cell. Often they slid cigarettes through the spyhole. Sometimes they got the head of the prison to hand over some apples to us. The head of the prison was a somewhat elderly

Italian. He was a jolly man and consoled us with the words: "You will all be home for Christmas."

A friend from the company with which I had previously served had to fetch my civilian clothes from home. Then I had to hand in my uniform. A week later the older man was taken away by the police. We did not know what would happen to him. We thought they would shoot him because he had already been sentenced to death.

One day, my youngest brother Anton visited me. He brought me some food and warmer clothes. But I was allowed to speak to him only under supervision.

A week later they took away my other two friends. I was left on my own in the cell. Now I was allowed to go out more frequently and I saw the priests more often as well. Bartholomäus Terzer, priest in Lazfons, and Father Polykarp, priest of Wangen am Ritten, who had given shelter to Canon Gemper at that time, took special care of me. Father Polykarp always comforted me with the words: "When we trust in the Lord God and pray diligently, he will not abandon us." The Father probably knew what was awaiting me, what a concentration camp meant. Being clergymen they were better informed.

The Journey to the Concentration Camp

After the third week in prison a guard from my previous company arrived one evening. He came into the cell and sat down on a bunk. He tried to be friendly and polite. He asked how I was and whether a clemency plea had been submitted on my behalf. But I was not aware of any such plea. Then he told me that he would have to take me to a court hearing in Munich the following day and that I would probably then be acquitted. He spoke to me in such an insistent and unctuous way that I almost looked forward to the following day. That same evening I also met Father Polykarp and told him the news. He promised to include me in his prayers and gave me his blessing. Immediately after the evening meal I crept under the blanket, because I wanted to get up early the following morning. But of course I could not go to sleep straight away because I was, after all, anxious about the next day. I could not help thinking of the three comrades who had been taken away before me.

I was woken up at six o'clock in the morning – it was the 15th of December. They gave me my suitcase. We had to be at the station at six-thirty. The guard had rather a lot of luggage and so, of course, I gave him a hand. It was cold and it was a long way to the station. We had hardly boarded the train when it pulled away. In the compartment I felt totally free, although the guard was sitting next to me. He held a newspaper in his hand and was reading it. He acted as if I was of no concern whatsoever to him. He smoked a cigarette and I was allowed to smoke one as well. Nobody could have guessed that I was a prisoner. Because he granted me so much freedom I trusted him completely. I really believed that I was on my way to the court hearing in Munich, as he had assured me. So the thought of escape never entered my head. I only wondered about what had happened to the other three, and whether I would ever see them again, or whether they had been removed from this world already. I hoped that I would suffer a better fate.

The train stopped in Merano. The guard got off the train with some other passengers and asked me to keep an eye on the luggage. He wanted to drink a cup of coffee in the bar. And so I remained on my own on my seat. The two older women, who sat opposite me, had probably not realized that I was a prisoner of this guard. Many questions and thoughts went through my mind. What was the meaning of all of this? Perhaps my escort was already waiting for me outside with a pistol in his hand. Where should I go? There was a lot of snow and so they would quickly track me down and arrest me. This would then have been the end.

I thought again about what my escort had told me the previous evening. While I was brooding over this, the train pulled off. My escort had not yet returned. I was determined to try to escape in case I should be left without a guard in Bolzano. But then I saw the guard come back. He looked at me straight away. He said that he had nearly missed the train and that he had lept on to the last carriage. He had bought himself a newspaper.

The train went on.

Soon it stopped again. What was wrong? Of course it was an air-raid alarm. It did not take long until we heard the enemy planes and the shooting of the flak. Immediately afterwards bombs rained down on Bolzano. We made very slow progress. It took us twelve hours from Schlanders to the Brenner Pass. We arrived at the border at seven in the evening. Up till then everything had gone well. At the Brenner Pass the journey became an ordeal for me. The train was stopped before it reached the station. They said that it could not go any further because the station had been bombed. The electricity had been cut off, and only a few street lamps and torches provided light. My escort had to find a way for us to move on. It was very cold and I was not equipped for the winter. But finally we reached Innsbruck. Many buildings had been destroyed. On the street in front of us there was an unexploded bomb. Again we had to wait until the street had been provisionally cleared. The city had been severely bombed that day. Many buildings had collapsed, including part of the barracks to which I had been assigned. When we arrived at the gate of the barracks my escort reported to the guard and said that he would pick me up the following morning.

Now an SS officer took charge of me. He shouted at me and asked whether I was a shoemaker. I was ordered to immediately remove the rag – he meant my blue apron which I wore as a man from the Sarn Valley. I took it off of course and put it in the pocket of my jacket. I had to go in front of him up the steps until we reached a long corridor with many doors on both sides. In every door there was a small spyhole. I was familiar with this from Schlanders. Everything in the corridor was spotlessly clean and brightly lit. I had to stop before the third or fourth door on the right. The SS man unlocked it and pushed me into the cell. I heard him say: "Enjoy yourself with that swine in there." The door fell shut behind me.

What I saw was terrible. A man of about thirty-five was sitting in the cell, chained to the floor, his clothes torn, his hair dishevelled and his face distorted with pain and fear. He was trembling all over. He looked at me so sadly and help-lessly that tears came to my eyes.

The cell was in semi-darkness. There was neither a bunk nor a chair in the room. There was a bit of straw on the floor. I sat down next to the man and noticed that his wrists were bleeding. He asked me to loosen the handcuffs a little. I did so in such a way that nobody would notice. Then he told me what had happened to him. He had deserted from the army and stayed in the forest near Innsbruck. That is where the police had tracked him down and taken him to prison. He was now seated, tightly chained to a ring secured in the floor. The siren had gone off at eleven o'clock. He heard the cell doors being opened and heard running and shouting in the corridor. Only his door remained closed. Not long after he heard the first planes. By this time the bombs had already been dropped. Suddenly there was a terrible crash and the windows broke with the air pressure; the glass fragments were flying around everywhere. He was badly shaken. Everything started shaking and he thought that the whole building would soon collapse. Finally the all-clear was given.

I gathered together a little straw in a corner, lay down, but could not sleep. It was cold in the cell and we had no blankets. Now I regretted for the first time that I had not tried to flee in Merano. When I thought about my fellow prisoner I was still content with my fate. He could not change his position at all and could not lie down. Outside in the corridor we could hear the guard walking up and down. I did not fall asleep until late at night, kept waking up and heard my fellow prisoner moaning. I think he was weeping. He had every reason to do so.

At six o'clock in the morning there was activity outside the cell. You could hear doors being unlocked and locked. Probably the cells were being cleaned, beds were being made and coffee was being handed out. But nothing happened outside our cell. I just hoped to be collected by my escort as soon as possible. But I kept hoping for quite a long time. My fellow prisoner became more and more unsettled. He was afraid of another bomb alarm. I started to become afraid as well that I might be killed by bombs in the prison. I kept praying that the Lord might spare me. At about ten o'clock sirens did in fact start to scream. In the corridor outside there was more shouting and running. Cell doors were opened and slammed shut, people were running along the corridor and down the steps. I heard a voice shout: "Is everybody downstairs?" I knocked several times on the door, but it was in vain.

There was a terrible silence. Then the planes could be heard droning and coming closer and closer. There was a sound of thunder and crashing, the floor shook, and again and again there was a gust of air. I was frightened that the whole building would collapse. I imagined how I would fall into the depths with the wooden beams and fragments of the wall, be crushed and draw my last breath. It was even worse to imagine being caught between the walls and dying slowly without being rescued.

I still do not know how long the alarm went on. It seemed to me to go on for ever. Finally the all-clear was given. After some time steps could be heard in the corridor. We were both happy to have escaped. When you think you are so close to death you come to appreciate life.

In the corridor food was being handed out, but they went past our door. My escort had our food for the journey and he simply would not turn up. I guessed that he would not be able to continue the journey with me, maybe because all the roads and rail tracks had been destroyed by aircraft attacks. Hours went by. In the afternoon I finally heard my escort's voice. I was looking forward to leaving. With a friendly look I said good-bye to my fellow prisoner. I felt great pity for him because there did not seem to any hope at all for him. I think that after the war I recognized him in a photograph, taken when he was being hanged.

My escort and I went by train to Hall. Since it was evening, he took me to the prison for the night. The cell was very clean. It contained a table, two chairs, a bunk with a sack of straw and two blankets. My escort supplied me with plenty of food. The prison guard appeared with a bowl of pea soup and enough bread. Of course I ate everything up. The guard's family was in Hall and he wanted to visit them.

Before I lay down for the night, he came back and asked me if there was anything I wanted. He told me a lot about his family. I also noticed that he wanted to tell me something, but just could not put it into words.

Finally he asked me, somewhat reluctantly, if I had money or any other valuables on me. He advised me to hand them over to him. In my astonishment I asked him why, and he broke it to me very gently that he had to take me to Dachau and that everything would be taken away from me there in any case. He asked me if I wanted to write a letter home. I said I wanted to do so and he brought me pen and paper. I gave him my wallet which contained eight hundred lire, a few photographs, a letter from my mother, a cigarette lighter, a tin of tobacco and a watch. He took these items and promised to send them home. I hid the cigarettes, a few matches and a rosary in the sleeve of my jacket.

Now I realized what was going on.

The escort had obviously kept the destination of the journey secret because he was afraid that I would then have tried to escape if he had told me in Schlanders. After all he was a good person. The letter I wrote was as follows:

Hall, 16th December 44

Dear parents,

I would like to write you just a few lines. I am on my way to Dachau, and I left Schlanders two days ago. I spent last night in Innsbruck and I saw and experienced some terrible things there. Today I felt terrified and desperate under a hail of bombs in the prison in Innsbruck, and now I am in the prison in Hall, where I will spend the night. In the meantime I could get an impression of what ten years in the concentration camp in Dachau will mean for me, because my escort hinted at what would await me there. He still gave me the opportunity to write to you. I would like to thank you sincerely, my parents, and everybody who has helped me, for everything, farewell, until we meet again at home or in ... Please pray for me and send my greetings to everyone who asks for me.

Your son Franz

That night I thought a lot about home, about my parents and brothers and sisters and about all my good friends. I had given up hope of ever returning home again. The letter was for me a farewell forever. I started to pray until, after some time, I nearly fell asleep at the table. Then I lay down.

When I woke up the next morning it was already light, as I could see through the small, narrow, barred window. Some time later the guard brought breakfast, coffee and bread, and a dish of water for me to wash myself. He did not say a word and bolted the door again. Late in the morning my escort came to collect me. At the station we got into a first-class compartment in which several SS officers were talking quite loudly about the political situation. We sat down in a corner; my escort lit a cigarette. When he saw that I also wanted to smoke, he gave me a firm push and said that I was not allowed to smoke in the presence of the officers. It would be forbidden for me. An SS officer asked my escort where he was taking me. He replied, almost hesitantly, to Dachau. Now all of them looked at me and one of them asked me, what mischief I had been up to. I answered:

"I did not enlist at the right time." He answered: "In Dachau you will certainly learn to obey orders." It became more and more clear to me that I could expect nothing good in Dachau. The train soon stopped, and once again bombs started to fall. It was only later in the afternoon that we approached Munich. One could see from the distance that the city was in flames. It had been bombed very severely that very day.

We got off at the station. There was total chaos there. My escort asked a policeman about something which I did not understand. The policeman walked ahead of us, over stones and the debris of houses which had collapsed, along a street to a big building. There I was allowed to use the toilet and then I had to go into a storeroom. The door was locked behind me. I looked around. There was cleaning equipment there and a stool to sit on. As I immediately guessed, these were my quarters for the night. I sat down on the stool and wanted to lean against the wall. But it was damp and cold. I could not lie on the floor either, because it was made of concrete and in addition it was wet. So I put my head in my hands and bent forward so that they rested on my knees. I sat there, a picture of misery. I was shivering from the cold. But even worse was the fear of what was to come. I would never get rid of this feeling of fear until my liberation on the 29th of April 1945.

I wanted to go to sleep in order to forget, at least for a short time, what I had been through in the last three days. But who could go to sleep in a situation like this? I dozed on and off and began to pray. Only this gave me comfort and hope. Few can imagine how long a night like this lasts. But even it went by.

I woke up in a start when I heard footsteps. The door was unlocked and the escort brought tea and a piece of bread. He left me on my own while I ate. Then I took my small suitcase and followed him. We went out into the open. There was not a cloud in the sky, but it was very cold. We went through the devastated streets to the station and looked for the train to continue our journey, our journey … to Dachau. We got in and the train pulled away after a lengthy wait. There were older women and soldiers in my compartment. No one spoke. We came to Allach, a village between Munich and Dachau. It had been heavily bombed that morning. The train stopped; a few people got off. That is when I saw some workers in striped uniforms clearing things away near the station grounds. SS guards were standing next to them. So these were the prisoners from Dachau.

The train made only slow progress and kept stopping. We arrived at a junction: the track on the left went to the town of Dachau, the one on the right to the concentration camp. We went to the right. In the distance houses and barracks could be seen. We passed some barracks and then the train stopped. There was no station; the tracks ended here. We got off. My escort asked one of the SS men who came out of another compartment how to get to the camp. He pointed straight at the camp gate. When we arrived there a group of eight to ten prisoners was marching briskly in step out of the gate.

They were all very thin, their faces were pale, their hair was close-cropped, their striped uniforms were sagging as if they were empty. They wore wooden shoes on their feet. SS men marched to their left and right. A sad sight, especially for me.

An SS man at the gate asked us what we wanted. My escort handed over a letter. When the SS man had read it, he sent us to a different gate. We walked along the camp wall, which was very high and had an electrified barbed-wire fence. We arrived at the gate, but because nobody opened it, we had to go all the way back again. The same SS man told my escort that he could now leave, and that he would certainly take care of me. I took a close look at my escort again. It was a silent, sad farewell.

Life in the Camp in Dachau

The entrance to the camp was through a house, the so-called "Jourhaus". There was a clock on the house; the time was eleven-thirty. Above the door was written in larger letters "Arbeit macht frei". We passed through the door which was immediately closed behind us. We turned right, passed a shed, and came to a room. An SS man pushed me inside. Two prisoners were already waiting there for me. I had to take off my clothes. One of them brought a large paper bag into which he packed the clothes. The other made an exact list of what had been put into the bag. Even the chain had to be removed from my neck. The bag was tied up with a string and labelled with my name and exact address. I was allowed to keep the socks and the braces. I was then shorn all over, probably because of the risk of lice. One could not be oversensitive when you were being shorn of your hair. Quite a few hairs were simply plucked out. In another room I was then photographed from all angles. An exact record was made of everything: name, date of birth, nationality and religion. When I said "Catholic" the SS man immediately made a pointed remark: "Now we will teach you to pray in a different way." I was given a worn-out shirt and underpants. When I saw myself in a big mirror I could not help laughing. The SS man took me to the bunker through a long corridor with many doors. He pushed me through one of them into a cell. I looked around. In the cell there was a bunk bed without a sack of straw or a blanket, a closet, a small washbasin and a radiator. The cell was spotlessly clean. A parquet floor, even white walls and ceiling, and a narrow tilting window with a very closely barred iron grid. The bunk bed was made from wooden boards, but in the middle a board was fitted in at right angles, which made it almost impossible to lie on it. The room was about three metres long, two metres wide and two and a half metres high. One did not freeze to death, but one froze. So I stood there for a time, completely shorn, starved, almost naked. It was the 18th of December. I sat down on the closet. This was the only place where you could sit normally. We draft resisters were separated from the large group of prisoners by the offices, the church and the washrooms. If you were allowed to leave the bunker cell, you were taken to a shed built on to the bunker at the end of the prison yard and shortly afterwards transported to an outlying camp. The treatment we enjoyed there was hardly better, actually worse than in the rest of the camp. This is why the prisoners called us the "bone men" whenever they saw us going in or out through the camp gate. This was the camp to which, as I now know, Josef Mayr-Nusser would have come had he not starved to death on the way there.*

While I was sitting around in the bunker cell, a door was unlocked and a shrill voice shouted: "Come out!" I heard

---

* Translators' footnote: Josef Mayr-Nusser, 1910–1945, was a leader of the South Tyrolian resistance against the Nazis. Both the author and Josef Mayr-Nusser, were awarded the honorary citizenship of Bolzano in 2010.

a few muffled steps, and the door was closed again. I saw that someone was looking through the spy hole in my door. Immediately after this my door was unlocked. An SS man stood in the doorway. I had already jumped up and was standing to attention in the middle of the cell. I was told to come out, I ran quickly and was already standing outside in the corridor. Opposite me I saw a man whose appearance was very much like my own. The two of us had to walk quickly, with the guard in front leading us, to the exit door. There was a small washroom on the right. We fetched brooms and buckets with water and rags. I quickly picked up a broom and a dustpan, because I thought it would be easier to use these rather than to mop. The guard immediately shouted at me: "You lazy bastard! You will soon learn what to pick up first." Saying this he slapped me. Then he tore the broom from my hand and ordered me to crouch down and to hold my hands stretched out in front of me. He put the broom in my hands. In this position I had to hop up and down the whole corridor twice. At the end of this I was totally finished and had to hand over the broom to my colleague. I was given a bucket with water and a rag. Within a short time we cleaned the whole of the extensive corridor. Then we had to go back into the cell.

When I was alone in the cell and had time to think, it soon became clear to me what I had done wrong before: you always had to jump at the hard job then you would be given an easier job. Suddenly I heard steps and the clanging of buckets and ladles. The steps came nearer and nearer to my door. The flap opening was unlocked and lowered so that it formed a small table, and the dishes and cutlery were put on it. I took the food. I was of course very hungry, because I had not eaten anything since about eight o'clock in the morning. Almost devoutly, I ate about half a litre of very thin pea soup. When I had finished I felt even more hungry than before. But one got used to such trivialities in the course of time.

I was very tired but did not dare to lie down before the light was turned off. At last it became dark. I lay down without a blanket on the floor and said my evening prayer. Then I fell asleep.

This was my first day in Dachau.

The following morning, at about seven o'clock, I heard them distributing the food in the corridor. They ladled milk coffee into my aluminium bowl, filling it half-way. I remained standing because I was hoping to be given some bread as well. But the man with the coffee canister shouted at me: "What are you still waiting for, bread perhaps? Shove off or I'll take away your coffee."

I drank the coffee, rinsed the bowl and also washed my face. I only had my shirt to dry my face. I sat down again on the closet lid. A few hours went by. Then again one could hear the steps of someone approaching. The door was unlocked and everyone had to run out. Then my door was opened too, and I also had to go into the corridor. The cleaning started all over again. This time it worked out better for me. I immediately jumped at the buckets and rags and fetched water while the other one swept before me. In a short time we had cleaned the floor. When we were taking the cleaning utensils into the washroom we suddenly heard shouting and ranting outside. At that very moment ten to twelve men came running in. They were all equipped in the same way: shorn, barefoot, in a shirt and underpants like us. They were followed by two SS men who kept beating them with rubber truncheons. From the cries for help and the swearing of the men being beaten I could tell immediately that they were Italians. The newcomers were pushed throught the door and I was put back into the cell as well. I soon got used to the guard who observed me through the spyhole.

After a time I heard groups of workmen marching past my window in the yard. Probably they were going for their midday meal in the barracks. I was also looking forward to the meal. I stood at the door and waited for the flap to open. I stood there for a while until it finally became clear to me that here the principle applied: "He who does not work does not eat." In our row of cells no food was distributed.

Again I had a lot of time to think about things. I was sure that Hitler would lose the war. But I was troubled by my concerns about what they would do with us before liberation. Returning home seemed to me to be more and more unlikely.

In the late afternoon there was more activity again. The door next to ours was unlocked and a shrill voice shouted: "Two men out." None of the Italians who were in there moved. They probably had not understood anything. After a few quick steps one could hear slaps. Two men were thrown out into the corridor, one after another. Then things really started. The guard shouted, ranted and handed out punches. When he had calmed down a little the corridor still had to be cleaned. From then on the cleaning of the corridor was the Italians' job.

In the meantime it was nightfall. The work crews marched into the camp. With a ravenous hunger I devoured my evening meal, beetroot soup. I licked the bowl so clean that I did not need to rinse it afterwards. But eating just increased my hunger. When the light went out I lay down again on the floor as close as possible to a small radiator which had been fixed to the wall. There was definitely no risk of being burnt by it. But I did not quite manage to fall asleep. I was freezing, it was winter after all and I had no blankets. In addition to the cold I was worried about the following day.

At about six o'clock breakfast was brought again. The coffee tasted very good although it was only murky water made from roasted barley without any sugar. Of course they left out lunch again. In the late afternoon an SS man turned up and handed me my socks and the braces for my leather trousers. I had to go with this man to the cell building attached to the barracks. Inside this building the storeroom for clothes was immediately on the right. Two prisoners were sorting the clothes. The guard ordered them to give me clothes and to take me to room twelve. Then he disappeared. I immediately put on the clothes which they had thrown at my feet. To my surprise the trousers and jacket were not striped, but they were instead Italian military clothes on which the letters KZ had been painted with white paint. I was also given a cap, shoes and a blanket. In room twelve I was handed over to the oldest man in the room. He explained to me the regulations which applied there and ordered me to follow them very strictly because every breach would be punished severely. He assigned me a spot where I could put my things. It was my bunk. It was only now that I had time to look around. Behind the door there was a table, and beside it were two bunk beds. On the right there were two other bunk beds. On the left it looked exactly the same. There were twelve beds in all. On the bunks there were sacks of straw. I sat down as best I could. You could not sit upright on the beds. When the senior inmate went out, I was cautiously asked by my colleagues where I came from and why I was there. Gradually I learnt that we came from five different countries: Italy, Austria, Germany, Russia, Switzerland. We had all committed the same offence.

In the corridor of our barracks a shrill whistling noise was heard. All the senior inmates had to rush to the entrance. There they were given army bread and a piece of fat. In the room the food was divided among the twelve of us. The thin slice of bread and the fat were like a feast for me. Never before had bread tasted so good. But unfortunately there was little of it. The talk in the room was of course about food, but then we talked cautiously about politics as well.

When the whistle sounded we had to line up in the corridor. There was a head count and then we went back into our rooms. I was looking forward to sleeping on the sack of straw with the blanket. After another shrill blast of the whistle we crept into our beds. A few SS men went through the rooms; the senior inmate had to stay up and report the exact number of prisoners. We then had to show them our feet as well. An exact check was made of whether they were really clean.

Immediately people started screaming in the room next door. The sound of blows was heard. Those next door had to run out into the corridor. There they had to hop up and down the whole length of the corridor several times in a crouched position, then wash their feet in the washroom and run back as fast as they could to their beds. Whether their feet were clean or not was obviously not of interest to the guards. In our room everything seemed to be in order. After a check the light was switched off. At last we could sleep.

The following day, early in the morning, a shrill whistle sounded again and a voice shouted: "Everyone get out of bed." We ran without our shirts to wash. The washroom was situated at the end of the barracks. One had to be really fast to get to a tap and a closet.

We always had to go there and back double quick. Making the beds was not a big job for us. The sack of straw was quickly fluffed up and the blanket was quickly folded. But they all had to be folded in exactly the same way. The shoes were placed in front of the bunk. Everything was kept in the most scrupulous order. One of us per room had to take it in turns to fetch and hand out the coffee. If there was something left, everyone would get a few drops extra. The milk coffee tasted delicious. Bread was handed out only in the evening. One of us had to sweep the room. Clearing up was always a punishment. There was a wide variety of punishments in the camp. The least severe was twenty squats. It was much worse if one had to hold a chair at the same time. Then there were twenty press-ups. If someone touched the ground he had to start from the beginning until he sometimes remained lying on the floor exhausted. That poor man then received several kicks, and blows to the head. You had to stand to attention to receive the blows to the head. Whoever winced or tried to dodge the blows received a worse beating.

That day it was our room's turn to clean the corridor. Fortunately it was not my turn because it did not take long until people started shouting outside. One the cleaners was dragged into the room by some men and beaten up ferociously. The men shouted: "He stole bread. We'll beat him to death, on to the rack with him." I could not yet figure what "rack" meant but I was soon to find out. The man was thrown on to the table, a blanket was put over his body and his arms and legs were held tightly. Two other men delivered in turn blows to his buttocks. The poor man himself had to count out loud up to twenty-five. Afterwards he had to remain standing to attention for quite some time in front of his bunk.

For the time being nobody in our barracks needed to work. Christmas was approaching. We were very curious about whether we would see or hear any signs of Christmas. Most of us thought we would not. But on Christmas Eve a little tree was put up in a corner of the corridor. It was decorated with brightly coloured strips of paper but it did not have any Christian symbols. To our surprise, at midday on Christmas day, we received, instead of the usual cabbage soup, three potatoes in their skins and some gravy. This was really a feast for us. Each one of us was with his dear ones at home in his thoughts. Nobody will forget such Christmases in the concentration camp. I had hoped that the war would be over by Christmas. I prayed for peace everyday, but surrendered myself to the will of God. On those festive days you would of course ask yourself sombre questions such as: "Will I ever celebrate Christmas at home again? What will happen in the future? Will I perhaps, like many others in

Dachau, lose my life due to of starvation or disease or as a result of being beaten to death?" After such thoughts only one thing helped and that was prayer. I would probably have despaired otherwise.

On the 26th of December we were informed that we would be taken to another camp, to Hersbruck. I thought I had got it wrong, because I had understood "Innsbruck". But unfortunately the place was really called Hersbruck, near Nuremberg, and not Innsbruck. Some looked forward to getting away from here, some however wanted to know whether life was even worse in other camps. So we looked to the future with concern.

On to Hersbruck

In the morning of the 27th of December the order came to decamp. This meant putting on shoes and lining up with a bowl and spoon in the corridor. The barracks were completely cleared. We had to march past the kitchen one by one and everyone received a slice of army bread, a piece of sausage and a piece of margarine. Nobody had any idea how long this supply would last. So we marched with these precious supplies in our hands out through the camp gate. Outside the train was ready and waiting nearby. We were loaded on to the cattle trucks, about thirty men per truck. Then the door was closed and carefully locked. High up in the truck, on one side, there was a small barred window. Because we were so hungry we all gave into the temptation to eat up all our provisions straight away, without knowing how long we would be without food. The train slowly rattled along. We lifted each other up to the window in order to look out. Although we were standing close together, warming each other a little, it was very cold in the train. Above all, our feet were freezing. The train was moving forward quite slowly.

Around midday there was the first air-raid alarm. The trucks remained stationary; the engine was uncoupled. The guards marched around the barred trucks. We heard the aircraft and the flak. After a while the all-clear sounded. Somebody hit the wall with his fist and shouted loudly that we had to relieve ourselves. The reply came from outside: "You dirty pigs, shit in the corner like a normal pig!" But we did not give up so quickly, and finally the door was opened. One after the other was allowed to get out and do his business behind the train under surveillance. We could also get a bit of fresh air, because the stench in the truck was unbearable. The train stood on a siding in a sparse pine wood. When we had been crammed back into the truck, hunger made itself felt again. In my case hunger had been gnawing at my stomach since my arrest. It was getting worse from day to day. It is impossible to imagine now what it was like.

Late in the afternoon the train engine moved on. After about an hour it became dark, and at about seven o'clock in the evening the train stopped. We noticed that we were in a station. The trucks were shunted again to a siding. Of course there was no evening meal. Some wanted to lie down, but that was not so easy. After some jostling each of us had at least a small spot where he could squat. This was how we spent the night, hungry and freezing. It was impossible to think about sleeping. We dozed away. At one point the sirens howled; we were startled but we did not need to change our position. Perhaps one or two of us wished to be released from our present and future misery by a bomb. For me prayer was the only thing which helped me to get thorough all of this.

At dawn we were allowed to get out of the trucks. It was snowing outside. When we continued our journey without any breakfast, of course, it was still snowing. At midday we came into a station. After a brief stop we went on again. It was already starting to become dark when we came to a halt after some time.

Voices could be heard outside. The trucks were opened and we had to get out. The place was dimly lit. In front of the trucks several SS men were standing and waiting impatiently for us. Our stop was not a proper station: there were only a few tracks with several trucks. We were in the vicinity of Hersbruck. We climbed up through a valley in marching order. At the top on the left a row of lights could be seen. As I discovered only later, there was a factory located there in which many of us were put to work. We marched more and more slowly. We were of course weakened because we had not eaten or slept for two whole days. The SS men were shouting and ranting. They hit the last of us in the column who could hardly keep up. Then a number of lights could be seen through the fog. We had reached our destination.

Between two buildings there was quite a small ditch with a very narrow bridge. When we marched over it, every fourth man received a small round loaf of bread and a little jam. In front of a bigger building there was a large square. We were counted carefully and allocated to different rooms. I was assigned to a room on the second floor. Bed rest had already been ordered when we entered the room. One or two men looked down from their bunk. Then there was a big surprise.

One of them shouted: "Hey, Franz, are you here as well now?" I immediately recognized the voice. It was Toni Königsrainer from the Passeier Valley, who, with his fellow countryman, Franz Hauser, had been taken here from the prison in Schlanders a week before me. Of course I was very happy to meet friends from South Tyrol here. I even forgot about my tiredness and hunger. I was assigned a bunk and I sat down on it as best I could. I grabbed my bread straight away. After two days and one night this was the first food: I ate with my whole body, with my thoughts, with my eyes, with my mouth and with my hands. The whole of me was absorbed with eating. It was unsalted black bread. The jam, which was not sufficient for all the bread, tasted very good. Then I went into the washroom, which was situated on the first floor. There I washed my face and hands.

After I had cleaned myself up a little, I returned to our room with my fellow travellers. I hoped to be able to sleep undisturbed. The evening roll-call had already taken place before our arrival. I undressed and crept into my bunk, on which there was a full sack of straw. I covered myself with the blanket which had been given to me, put my trousers and jacket on top of it and stuffed my socks as a precaution under my head because socks were in short supply. Then I immediately fell asleep.

At six o'clock in the morning we were woken by a shrill whistle. Everybody ran without their shirts into the wash-room. If someone was caught with his shirt he was taught a lesson. So he had, for example, to take everything off, was then hosed down with ice-cold water and scrubbed with a brush until his body was bleeding. Or he was beaten with a rubber hose for so long until his back was covered with weals.

In the washroom there was a long basin with several taps, opposite the closet room, with about half a dozen bowls in a row. We had to really hurry up because those who were last always received some kicks. When the SS were not there themselves, the senior inmates or another "important" person saw to our daily harassment. After returning to the dormatory we made our beds. Then the senior inmate handed out coffee. We had to line up in the yard and there was a careful head count. The various fatigue parties were then called out. They marched in step, singing a song, as they went to work. We newcomers had to assemble in the anteroom of the office. Inside I was asked for my name, place of birth, domicile, offence and tariff. Everything was documented. Finally I had to undress, was measured and weighed. When I stood on the scales I was shocked: in Schlanders I had weighed sixty-nine kilos, but now, after thirteen days, I was only fifty-nine kilos. If it went on like this I would soon be done for.

On our first day here we did not have to go to work. We even received a midday meal. It consisted of a thin pea soup which even tasted a little of meat. The midday soup was taken to where the fatigue parties were working by French prisoners-of-war on a horse-drawn sleigh.

When we had all eaten our supper we were allowed to talk undisturbed in the dormatory. I was immediately surrounded by South Tyrolians. Most of them came from the Passeirer Valley, Toni Königsrainer, Franz Hauser, Georg Oberprantacher, Franz and Heinrich Haller as well as Simon Dorfmann from Garn near Latzfons in the Eisack Valley. All of them wanted to get the news from me. Above all they were interested in finding out whether the war would soon be over. I did not know that myself. I was interested in life here. They could not give me any good news. From dawn to dusk it was hard labour, at midday there was a half-hour break, just enough time to eat the soup.

Now a shrill whistle sounded and a voice shouted: "Out for head count!" Then the running and sprinting started. Some were looking for fleas, others had already lain down on the straw sacks and fallen asleep. They were of course the last to make it to the yard. They received thumps from all sides. We had to line up in rows of three. If the row was not absolutely straight, our formation was broken up, and we had to lie down, get up, lie down, crawl around in the snow and then line up again in rows of three. Everyone wanted to stand in a straight row, but it happened nevertheless that we were repeatedly subjected to these harassments two, three times. When we had finally lined up succcessfully, the head count started. This usually turned out to be even more difficult because the foreigners did not understand German and had difficulty in calling out the correct number. If the German speakers had problems with counting the numbers, it was, of course, all the more difficult for the Italians, Croatians, Romanians etc. Often we had to start again two or three times from the beginning. When we finally succeeded, we were dismissed and allowed to return to the barracks. But when the guards were in a very bad mood and the roll-call was not a brilliant success, the whole group was harassed even more: standing to attention in the biting cold for hours at a time or crawling around in the snow, then standing up, lying down again, etc. This procedure sometimes lasted rather a long time.

If someone made a mistake during the head count he had to step out of the line, was beaten up until he was completely finished. Only then was he allowed to step back into the line again. When it was finally time to creep under the blankets we immediately fell asleep. Every day two men had to take turns to sweep the room. If you thought that you would be left in peace then, you were mistaken. Before that there was the "showing of feet" and everything that went with it. In spite of the plague of lice and our hunger we soon fell asleep because we were so exhausted.

Often I dreamt about home, but usually only bad things. I dreamt that I was on the run and was being hunted by the police – until I woke up in terror and was brought back to reality, which was even worse than the dream.

On the second day after our arrival I marched to a work site with the others. I was assigned to a construction troop. After twenty minutes we reached the building site, a very flat area, surrounded by small hills with a very sparse pine wood. On the site there were barracks with work tools and concrete, and next to this there was a big heap of sand. You could tell from all the foundations and pits that several more barracks were to be built here. A road that was paved with granite stones ran right through the middle of the area We had to go to work in small groups; I had a pickaxe and a shovel, others had iron bars. We probably had to hew the stones after they had been blasted from the rock. Of course we were accompanied by SS guards.

As there was about twenty centimetres of fresh snow, we first of all had to clear this away. We had to load the hewn stones with our bare hands on to the sledge, which was then pulled by a French prisoner-of-war to the building site. If the foreman of the troop was reasonably humane, and if the

SS guards were not exactly bad-tempered, we were allowed to clap our hands and warm them a little. It was strictly forbidden to put them in your pockets. Standing still was also forbidden. But we did not ever stand because we wanted to prevent our feet from freezing. At twelve o'clock we had a short midday break, then we were driven back to work and at about five o'clock we marched back to our living quarters. Then came the roll-call and the handing-out of the food. The time when we could chew our bread was the best part of the whole day. In our thoughts we were already eating it before we had even received it. In our thoughts we continued eating it afterwards, until the plague of lice became excruciating.

On this first working day I was very tired as I was no longer used to hard labour. All my limbs hurt, particularly my hands, which were covered in blisters. I lay down on the bunk, but fought against falling asleep because I did not want to be one of the last at the head count. Before falling asleep in the late evening I thanked the Lord God for being spared from greater harassment.

So the first days went by in Hersbruck without any major incidents. New Year came but our hopes for a day off work were disappointed. On New Year's Day itself we had to replace the rubble mill with our hands. We had to break the fist-sized granite stones with careful blows down to small road metal. I was tormented by home-sickness. I was increasingly preoccupied with constant desolate thoughts about our future. The only comfort I kept finding was in prayer. I pitied the people who had no faith and who thought that the whole of life was meaningless and hopeless. No wonder some of them took their own lives.

One week might have passed when, on a Sunday, we had to line up in the yard with our blankets, instead of going to the work site. In the night ten centimetres of snow had fallen. We had to beat our blankets in groups of two, on a field. When we were finished with this we had to do exercises in groups: get up, lie down, get up, lie down, forward and backward, right and left, and in the end we had to have a snowball fight. In the barracks we were given some thread to sew on our buttons and mend holes. Some people made gloves from rags.

In the afternoon writing paper was handed round. We were allowed to write home. But the letter was not allowed to have more than fifteen lines. But what could you write? Certainly not the truth. I wrote the following:

Dear parents,
At the beginning of my letter let me send you my sincere greetings ... So far I am fine, I have good work colleagues and there are also some South Tyrolians with me. ... I work in a quarry. How are you and my brothers and sisters? ... Give my best wishes to all who ask for me and please pray for me.
Your son Franz

You could not write more if the letter was to be forwarded. Probably it was even better if the people at home did not learn too much.

The afternoon ended rather desolately for me. I was homesick and had to cry. The letters were collected and brought to the censor's office.

On the 6th of January we were ordered to undergo delousing. We had to take off our clothes, which were then put into the steam boiler. Then we were taken to the shower room and locked in. Each one of us had been given a small flannel. At the beginning the water was very cold, but it then got warmer. It was a real blessing to be able to wash yourself properly for once. We were even allowed to use a piece of soap. After the shower we were given clean shirts and underpants. We had to replace the missing buttons with a nail or a piece of wood. Our clothes were still steaming and my leather braces had shrunk quite a lot.

In the afternoon it was back to work again. The Christmas and New Year holidays were definitely over.

The following days and weeks actually passed quite quickly. There was not time to be bored. We were preoccupied with worrying about what the next few hours would bring.

One day, I had to stay behind in the camp with three other comrades while the others were taken to work. We were taken behind a storeroom by an SS man. There was a dead prisoner lying there. Probably he had died the previous day as a result of hard labour and starvation, perhaps even as a result of a serious assault. It was a seventeen- to eighteen-year-old boy, who was just skin and bone. He lay there, curled up and frozen stiff. We had to carry him on a wide board to a tiny church situated on a slope. Because we could not admit to being Christians we could not look into the little church.

It was regarded as an exception if a prisoner was buried privately by his relatives. But our dead prisoner came from this area. So his relatives received permission from the head of the camp, Riegler. Normally the dead were hastily buried in a mass grave or taken to the crematorium.

On a Sunday at the end of January we had to line up in the morning in the yard and go in turns in pairs to the camp registry. There the name, date of birth and nationality of each of us were registered. We had to take off our clothes and were measured once again. I knew from Schlanders that I was 1,72 m tall. Now I was 1,70 m. So you also lost height here. When I heard that I weighed forty-five kilos, I thought at first that I heard incorrectly. But the man repeated what he had said. The comrade behind me, an Italian, weighed even less, forty-four kilos. When we left the room we looked at each other. We both shook our heads. We simply could not believe that we were so run-down. I thought that I had reached the survival limit, but it was going to get a lot worse, as I will report later.

My physical decline made me very thoughtful. I was all the more pleased to hear the surprising news that the young men under twenty, and twenty-five kilos underweight, would receive extra food. Since I was one of them. I actually received a quarter of a loaf of bread every Wednesday and many envied me for this. Nonetheless I continued to suffer from hunger like all the others.

Then there was another affliction which drove me almost to despair: scabies which caused terrible itching all over my body. I scratched myself day and night. My whole body was covered with sores. When I squeezed my skin, blood and pus came out. My underpants and shirt became quite sticky. My colleagues increasingly avoided me. The dirt was the perfect breeding ground for vermin and diseases. I noticed myself that I was becoming weaker by the day. It pained me of course that my best friends increasingly avoided me. In order to avoid becoming infected nobody wanted to come in contact with me. Finally I could not bear it anymore, physically and mentally. I asked the senior inmate to have me seen by a doctor. Such requests were made reluctantly because if somebody did not seem to the doctor to be sufficiently ill he received a severe punishment.

So I attended the appointment the following morning. There were several prisoners with various illnesses. When I had undressed and went up to the doctor he shouted at me and asked what was wrong with me. I explained to him my itching problem. He looked me up and down, his eyes became bigger and bigger and he shouted: "You pig, you dirty pig! Why didn't you report this sooner?" Then he immediately turned to the next person, looked him up and down as well and railed at him. He wrote a few lines on a piece of paper and sent us into the next room to a prisoner who was supposed to treat us. He began to spread a thick, oily-smelling fluid over the whole of our bodies. Then we received fresh clothes and were allowed to return to the barracks. Hardly anybody can imagine what a blessing it was to wear clean clothes once again. The two of us, who suffered from scabies, did not have to march out to the building site that day. We were kept busy in the camp yard and treated again in the evening with the ointment. In the evening I of course fell asleep immediately.

Every day after work I had to go to the clinic barracks to be treated. After three, four days I noticed that my affliction was clearly becoming better. After one week I was cured of the scabies. I now rediscovered my zest for life. My friends came up to me again.

One evening, when the senior inmate summoned two of us for the evening shift, I heard my name being called out. Being half asleep I could not get out quickly enough and was afraid I would be beaten. He called my name out again. In spite of this I did not move, but somebody gave away my bunk to him. The next moment he pulled the blanket from me. I jumped out. "You shirker, you wanted to dodge work!" And he immediately started to slap me. I then had to squat, hold out my hands, take the broom in my mouth and hop around the bunk in the middle of the room until I could hardly go on. The other man was allowed to return to his bunk. I had to clear up on my own. It was only when I was lying on my bunk again that I had time to recover from the shock. My teeth hurt terribly.

Something similar happened to me, when, after the mid-day meal, I went to get a second helping, in other words, some of the soup that was left. An SS man who did not know me noticed me and hit me. Such things happened hour after hour, day after day. When someone tried, for example, to warm his hands in his trouser pockets during work and was caught doing this, he had to hold, for hours on end, his pick and shovel crosswise on his shoulders, without any gloves or socks, at ten to twelve degrees below zero. Or when someone was pushing the wheelbarrow too slowly, his punishment was to rush around at the double with a heavily laden barrow on the camp square and to be kicked as well after this. If somebody ever caught the eye of one of the SS men he was beaten for any reason, however trivial. When I had escaped from the group of those under close surveillance, one of my best workmates got it. One day he was in a hurry and forgot to take off his shirt quickly before washing. For that he was treated with a brush and cold water. After that we did not see him anymore.

One day I was the last to collect my food. We had potatoes in their skins. The cook, a South Tyrolian by the name of Max Prantl from Merano, did not spoon me out the usual two or three potatoes, but eight to ten. Delighted, I ran to the semi-constructed barracks in which we were eating, and enjoyed my wonderful meal. I am grateful to the cook even to this day. When there were potatoes we ate them with their skins. In addition we tried to steal the skins from the tables of the SS men. In doing this we had to proceed very carefully because it was forbidded to eat their left-overs.

One evening the senior inmate announced to me that I had to go to the head of the camp the following morning. I was shocked because news like this usually bode no good, but meant disciplinary transfer to harder work, a move to another camp or being sent to the camp bunker, which was situated right behind the door to the dormitory. This bunker was a 2 by 1.5 metre small cage with wooden poles from the ground to the ceiling. The narrow opening had a sturdy lock. Instead of a bunk there was only a little straw on the floor; a bucket in the corner had to serve as a closet. The prisoners sometimes received something to eat only every four days. If I could I avoided walking past the bunker because the prisoners looked out so desperately between the poles.

Small Signs of Hope

The following morning I was ordered by an SS man to follow him. We went out through a gate and entered a small, clean room in the building next door, which served the head of the camp as an office. He sat behind a small table. After the SS man had introduced me, he saluted and left the room. The man behind the table, a high-ranking SS officer, looked at me with a smile. He had probably realized that my knees were shaking. I was allowed to sit on a chair and my fear disappeared. I had not heard an SS man speak to me in such a friendly way before. He asked where I came from and wanted to know exactly from which region of South Tyrol. He said he did not know the Sarn Valley, but that he had been in Merano quite often. As he came from Hall in Tyrol he had often visited South Tyrol. I had to give him details of the reason for my arrest. The head of the camp listened to me patiently and asked a few brief questions from time to time. Now and again he looked at the letter which he had lying in front of him. He smiled and nodded. It seemed to me that he took pity on me. He asked if anyone had applied for a pardon on my behalf. I knew nothing about this. Then he told me that my sentence had been commuted from ten to two and a half years in the concentration camp. He was pleased, he said, to be able to tell me this. He encouraged me to keep going so that I could one day return to South Tyrol.

Tears ran down my face, not so much because of the commutation, but because of the humanity which this man let me feel. I could have embraced him for joy. I thanked him and went out through the door. Outside the SS man was waiting for me and took me back to the work site.

After that I was no longer frightened of the head of the camp. But I was frightened of the Oberscharführer, who was the deputy in charge of our outer camp. The head of the camp visited only once every two to three weeks. That is when the Oberscharführer became nervous and began, out of sheer fear, to harass us. The preparation for the visit was worse than the whole visit itself.

When I returned to my workmates, they looked at me with curiosity. We were not allowed to speak, but they could all tell from my facial expression that nothing bad could have happened to me.

In the midday break I told them briefly what had happened and they all were just as pleased as I was. In the following months such commutations were announced repeatedly. We did not know the exact reasons for this. But probably many Nazis back home, now that the war would soon be over, who had delivered people to the concentration camp, were afraid of the retribution which awaited them. With these commutations they probably wanted to lessen the wrath of the homecomers.

At about midday every day two or three small planes flew close by us. We would not have thought anything of this if we had not heard two shots in the far distance one day.

We thought at first that a prisoner had escaped. The guards became nervous and we had to return to the work camp right away. There we lined up one by one beside the other group. The guard reported to the duty officer that the quarry group was fully mustered. There was another head count but nobody was missing. None of the guards answered the question of the duty officer about who had fired the shot. At this moment another plane flew past, and after a few seconds there was a crashing noise. The guard became even more nervous. The officer went with two men in the direction from which the crashing noise had come. We had to remain standing to attention in line. It was only after about ten minutes that we learnt what had happened. The guard who accompanied the man who brought the food trolley had realized that these were enemy aircraft and had fired two shots. As a consequence of this the pilot had turned round and fired back. The shots from the planes had missed their intended target and had hit our soup vat instead of the guard. Our midday meal was gone.

In the following days we were ordered not to move at all when planes approached. We were only too pleased to do so. Of course we were not frightened of enemy planes.

When the new camp was ready to be occupied and when we had cleaned and tidied everything up, the head of the camp and some SS officers arrived. We prisoners and the guards were standing in line. The Oberscharführer was very nervous. He kept marching up and down in front of us. Then the new rooms were inspected. After that we even received a better meal: milk soup with maccaroni. The gentlemen of the SS stood a little apart and watched how greedily we devoured the food. When I left the kitchen with my soup, a man came up to me with a spoon in his hand and asked me to give him a spoonfull of soup. He would give it back to me immediately afterwards. When I went up to him later he chased me away and I was the one who was cheated. A spoon of soup was at that time so valuable that I still have an exact memeory of it, a good forty years later. Those who were lucky enough to work in the kitchen had the opportunity to take something with them to the barracks from time to time. A South Tyrolian always brought salt with him and sprinkled a little of it on the unsalted slice of bread for his friends. As a fellow countryman I also dared one day to ask him for a pinch. But he rejected me rudely. So even then the solidarity of the South Tyrolians was not exactly exemplary.

One day, after the inspection of the camp, we moved to the new camp. This did not mean a lot of work for us because, apart from our very inadequate clothes, we possessed nothing. Some wore wooden sandals which consisted of boards the size of a foot with wires fastened over the top. Almost all of us owned a knife to cut up the bread. It was simply a piece of tin found somewhere on the building site and shaped and sharpened on a brick. So we marched for the last time out through the gate of the old camp, away from this lousy hole in which the bugs had almost driven us to despair during the night. Marching always was a bit of a problem. Almost everyone was limping because of an injury or frostbite. If somebody stumbled and fell he was kicked. When we were marching we always had to sing, sometimes even Tyrolian songs, but usually dirty songs, the kind the

SS enjoyed. When the guards noticed that someone was not joining in there was a hail of blows.

In the new barracks not everything was laudable. We had more room as we were accommodated in two-story bunks, but we froze all night. There was a small coal and wood stove in the middle of the barracks, but it was far from being adequate to heat the room. Another disadvantage of the new camp was that we had only one common washroom and toilet. In addition it was situated away from the barracks and it was not so easy to get to it at night. You always had to put on clothes for this. So some people preferred to relieve themselves right in front of the barracks. When the SS man was unable to find out who had done this the whole company was punished. After we had made our way back through the cold snow, it was very difficult to warm ourselves in bed.

One afternoon, shortly after we had moved into the new camp, I felt a slight chill. At first I did not think anything of this and continued working. Towards the evening the chill became worse. I started to have diarrhoea. And so I lay, a little heap of misery, shivering on my bunk. Sleep was out of the question. I looked forward to a warm coffee in the morning and hoped to get rid of the chill again with a warm drink and with the work. In spite of the coffee the chill got worse at the morning roll call. I did not dare to report that I was ill and went with the others to the quarry. During work I had to keep going to relieve myself. As I had to ask the guard each time, he noticed my condition. He exempted me from work. I became more and more miserable. I did not even enjoy the midday soup. And so I requested the Kapo to take me to the hospital block after all.

The guard gave me a thermometer and wrote down my name, date of birth, nationality and tariff. I had over thirty-nine degrees fever and was admitted to the block. The guard took me to a room with six bunks, of which three were occupied. The men who were lying there did not move. To me they seemed like dead men. I took off my clothes and lay down. A linen sheet was even spread out over the sack of straw. Fortunately there was a closet in the block because I had to relieve myself constantly. Afterwards I always felt so miserable that I just dozed on. In that room we had our peace and quiet. We did not disturb each other because we were too weak to move. In the evening an SS guard went through the block and did a head count. Then we were left undisturbed until the morning. When it was already light, to my surprise, a Red Cross nurse came into our room. She went from patient to patient and took their temperature. But she did not utter a single word. I had the impression that she was a foreigner. When this somewhat older person had finished taking our temperature she gave each of us a tablespoon of ground coal. She fetched a plate with a syringe on it. I had to uncover my left arm. She tied my upper arm with a strip of cloth. After she had taken blood from me and from the others as well, the woman left again. I felt so miserable that day that I thought my life was over.

Almost Finished at Twenty

It was the 6th of March, 1945, the day on which I became twenty. At a point when life normally really begins for someone I would have to leave this earth. I felt like the most forlorn of the forlorn. There was no help in sight anywhere. My neighbours in the next beds had to endure the same fate; they could not help me either. There was no word of consolation from anyone; no friend, no brother, no sister, no father, no mother was there. Would they never see me again in this life? I was overcome with homesickness and I wept. Then I prayed and left myself in the hands of the Lord God. The best priest could not have prepared me for death better than my present desolate situation. I forgave all those who had had me brought here.

At midday they gave us a little millet gruel. I was too weak to eat. After a few spoons I fell back on to the bunk. I did not feel hungry any more. The man next to me stared very greedily at my soup and so I gave it to him. He had already overcome the crisis. My thoughts and dreams were all confused. Then I realized that I had to relieve myself. But while I was trying to work out how to get to the closet, I had already done it in my trousers. So I was now lying in my own faeces and could not call on anyone to help me. Soon I forgot my dirty bed, and lost consciousness. I did not come round again until the following morning when the Red Cross nurse (this time it was a different one) asked me how I was. I felt a bit better than the day before. It was only when I had eaten my portion of coal that I noticed that two roommates had gone. I thought they had got over everything. Although I was no longer afraid of dying, and sometimes even yearned for death, I still hoped for freedom and to return home. The nurse brought us another chamber pot at my request. I asked the man in the next bunk what had happened to the other two patients. He told me that they had been carried away by prisoners on stretchers the previous evening during the head count. He did not know whether they had been still alive, but probably they were not. The only thing that distinguished the living from the dead was the movement of the chest wall during breathing and the eyes which were often looking for help.

I thanked God that I was still alive.

That day I managed to eat my soup with short periods of rest. At one moment you are so full of life and hope, and a little later you feel desperate again. Between the head count in the evening and the morning you could recover, but also die.

In the morning the young Red Cross nurse was sent to us again. She was probably supposed to learn on us how to take blood, because she missed four to five times when she put the needle in. She became nervous and finally had to get the older nurse. Every day we were afraid of having our blood taken. We realized that the nurse did not intend to torment us; perhaps she had only been forced to do this work by the SS. We had our doubts about whether she was actually a nurse at all.

From now on I felt better every day. I had overcome the lowest point. However my recovery progressed only slowly because we received no medication apart from the coal.

I think that those of us in the outer camps, particularly in the smaller ones, were better off than those in the main camp. Probably not every brutal order reached us, or it was not carried out unless it was an SS monster who was head of the camp. And in that respect we were favoured by good fortune, because our head of the camp had retained some human feeling. Had I been in Dachau with my scabies, they would certainly have transported me with other sick comrades to the gas chambers, and the same would have happened now with my dysentery. In the smaller camps they were not equipped with transport vehicles and were also too far away from the gas chambers. Dysentery was a disease which in the final months of the war carried away thousands. My bedmate and I hoped that we would escape this fate after all.

But for me there was a further affliction. My toes started to hurt more and more. When I examined them more closely one day, I noticed that the tips of some of the toes of both feet had turned black and blue, in other words were frostbitten. Many of us suffered from frostbite. And this was not surprising because we had to to walk around the whole day in the snow, barefoot, in extremely poor shoes with holes in them at ten to fifteen degrees below zero. It was anything but a pleasure to slip barefoot into the stiff and frozen shoes every morning. If you were lucky and the shoes were a bit too big, you could wrap a cloth rag or a piece of cement sack around your feet. Toilet paper was greatly in demand for this purpose. It was also used mainly to bandage wounds. Each one of us received one metre of it a week. It was needed least of all for its real purpose. I reported my foot problem to the Red Cross nurse. She brought me an ointment for frostbite, which I was supposed to apply once a day. The pain became worse nevertheless. Walking, in particular, became a torment.

If somebody from home had now seen me, he would not have believed that I would come out of this camp alive. I looked like a walking corpse. Just skin and bone, with our faces contorted with pain and our eyes embedded deeply in their sockets, my comrade and I walked up and down the corridor of the barracks, holding on to the walls. After a short time we crept, dead-tired, under the blanket again. On the sixteenth day after our admission to the sick block we were discharged. We had in the meantime recovered sufficiently to be able to stand without anyone having to hold on to us. In clothes which were much too big, our blankets rolled under one arm, our eating bowl in one hand, our spoons in a pocket, we walked unsteadily from the block to our barracks. We had mixed feelings. On the one hand we were looking forward to meeting our previous workmates again; on the other hand we were frightened to return to daily life in the camp, with everything that it involved.

It was late in the afternoon. The work troops which were not on night shift marched into the camp. In the camp itself there were only a few workers left, only those who were no longer of any use for work in the mines. I too was assigned to them. There were a few minor jobs to be done in the camp, which were supervised by a civilian master builder.

We five, six men were assigned to him. Fortunately the sun was shining; indeed it was very warm. That did us a lot of good. We were looking forward to the approach of spring. In the camp we were not always watched by the guards. The civilian worker himself displayed little enthusiasm for work and treated us in a sympathetic way. I had the impression that some guards no longer displayed any pleasure in torturing us unnecessarily.

The front came nearer and nearer and to our delight there was an air-raid alarm every morning. It often lasted two, three hours. We were allowed to rest in the barracks. Sometimes the alarm lasted longer and so our midday meal was delayed. But we gladly put up with this. The guards always became nervous. We saw the bombers flying high in the sky and heard the flak. We often heard the bombs as well which fell on Nuremberg, because the city was not very far away from us. Several times a day low-flying aircraft approached and whizzed just over the roofs of the barracks. We had to remain completely still in the barracks. The guard looked outside very cautiously through a gap in the wall. Once the low-flying aircraft took us by surprise during our midday meal. We prisoners were busy eating and the SS guards were standing in the camp street. Suddenly there was a terrible crash. We could still hear the plane flying off into the distance. When we thought that the coast was clear we dared to go out into the street. An SS man was being carried off by two others into the SS barracks. One SS man had been severely injured and two others had been slightly injured. We were scared, but had ourselves escaped. Three barracks had been damaged.

"You Can Become Soldiers"

At the end of March a rumour went round that we would be discharged and sent to the front. And one day we did in fact have to line up on the parade ground. In front of us stood the SS men we knew and some SS officers we did not know. One of the latter made a short speech, but in a tone of voice which was totally unfamiliar to us. "As you have proved yourselves at work the Führer wants to pardon you and you can fight as soldiers for the Führer on the front ..."

We were pleased that we were being addressed, for once, as human beings. We were also pleased about the chance to get away from here, never mind where to. Although I could not have much hope for myself in my condition – I could hardly stand up – I waited with curiousity nonetheless. The SS men went to the other side of the square, and the ones who were called out had to run over to them at the double. Whoever managed somehow to get over there, remained there and was fit for the front.

My workmate, Simon Dorfmann, managed to do this fairly well. I resolved with my last effort (one could hardly say "strength") and a strong will to get over to the other side quickly. But the saying – "where there is a will there is a way" – could not be realized in this case. The will was there, but the way was too hard. I had hardly taken ten steps when I felt that my legs would not carry me any further. Half-way across I sank to the ground. I wanted to pick myself up again right away, but I could not. I simply had to rest for a little. When I finally stood up again with great effort and tried to continue running, I was given a signal and sent back. I stepped back sadly to rejoin those who had not managed it despite their efforts to use their last reserves. As a result of this physical examination, about a third of the prisoners were declared fit for military service. They were aged between twenty-five and forty. We young men of twenty and below were the worst off. Those who were fit left us the following day. We were the sad ones who were left behind.

Work in the camp was no longer so hard and we were no longer under constant guard. We just pretended to have something to do. The weather was pleasant. If it had not been for the terrible hunger we could even have recovered. The swede soup became thinner and thinner. The weekly piece of extra bread for us very young ones was no longer handed out either – now when I would have needed it the most.

The front came closer and closer. We heard shooting day and night. There were repeated air-raid alarms. The guards stopped harassing us. We hoped to be liberated soon. But the fear still remained of what would await us when we were left to the enemy.

At the beginning of April we heard that we would soon be transported back to Dachau. Of course we would have preferred to stay where we were. We were very afraid of

Dachau, as well as of the journey there under these circumstances. I was actually never without fear and I think it was not much better for the others. From the first day in the concentration camp until our liberation we carried a heavy burden.

Back to Dachau

In the morning of the 4th or 5th of April, after breakfast, we had to line up in the yard to decamp. The only things we were to take with us were our eating bowls. After several head counts we marched off. The guards seemed to be in a great hurry. They kept driving us on. It was very hard for me to keep up; my frostbitten feet were very painful. But if I wanted to survive, I had to keep going. I was in too good a shape to be transported with those who were sick; I had after all been discharged from the sick block. When we came down from the new Habburg camp to Hersbruck station they were already waiting for us. We had another head count and then we were herded into the empty cattle trucks. The trucks, with fifty men in each, were securely bolted.

When the train started to move, each of us tried to look out through the small window to see where we were going. I chose for myself a spot on the floor so that I could rest a little. But I soon had to get up again, because otherwise my fellow prisoners would have trampled me to death. Finally I found a spot far away from the window.

Midday came. But we hoped for food in vain. Instead low-flying aircraft came by. The train stopped. In the distance we heard a siren. Soon there were also bombers thundering high above us. The train stopped on the track in an unremarkable village. We did not know how far we had travelled. Some of us wanted to relieve ourselves, but however persistently we knocked and beat on the truck door, it did not help. Each of us had to do his business where he happened to be standing. After sometime everything trickled through the floor. It was impossible to sit or lie down because there was not enough room. Finally the sky seemed to be clear again and the train started moving once again. It moved forward quite slowly. In the late afternoon we stopped again. One by one the truck doors were opened. We were able to relieve ourselves and get some fresh air. The train was standing on the main track, concealed on the one side by bushes and on the other by a hill. One had to be careful because the tracks were being almost constantly bombed by low-flying aircraft. The sun was still shining; it was a wonderful day for everyone who was free. When I went behind a truck I saw a dead prisoner lying there. I looked more closely and recognized in him my previous workmate who had been, some time ago, hosed down in the washroom with icy water and scrubbed almost to death with a brush, and whom none of us had seen since then. Probably he had been lying up to now in the sick block and had died a miserable death during the transport. Now they had simply thrown him out of the truck. While I was still standing there I heard somebody shout: "Everyone take cover!" I saw some of the SS men throwing themselves under a truck. I took refuge between two trucks and the planes were already roaring past us. Probably they had not noticed us at all, or too late. We were driven back into the trucks, but before we were all inside the planes came roaring back and flew in a loop very close above us. While they were roaring over us at an angle they fired at the guards.

The noise was terrible. The guards who were standing in a circle in front of our truck threw themselves quick as a flash on to the ground. Morevoer the last compartment of the train, where the guards were, was hit by the gunfire. Through the open door I saw two SS men lying on the ground. One of them was bleeding severely from a head wound and was trying to pick himself up. The other was rolling on the ground. Clearly both were severely injured. The SS men rushed to bolt the doors of our trucks again. Afterwards we learned that our guards had shot back at the first of the two planes. These turned round in response and flew back to take revenge. This was a good lesson for our guards. After that they did not shoot back with their guns, however low the planes were flying.

When it became dark, the train moved on again. Sleep was out of the question. We could neither sit nor lie down. I was very tired and finally I managed to squat. I was very afraid of feeling sick. Anyone who sank unconscious to the floor had hardly any chance of getting up again and of being taken along with the rest of us. The dead were thrown out of the train at the following stop.

Of course many of us wanted to settle down on the floor. There was a lot of frantic pushing around, grumbling, cursing and ranting. But all this did not help, and the room did not become any bigger as a result. Because it was as dark as in a sack you did not know who was next to you.

I could not help thinking of my workmate who had been thrown out of the truck, either dead or at least half-dead. He had been a year younger than me and we had become good friends. He too had suffered greatly from homesickness. I had thought that he had died after his cruel treatment in the washroom. I would have wished so much for him that he could have seen once again the loved ones he had so yearned for. And now, after all the hardships of life in the camp, he had been thrown out of the train like a piece of wood during the transport back to Dachau.

I will never forget these images.

Late at night the train stopped. We heard the train engine move off. We had obviously been shunted on to a siding. We might have to wait there for hours or days. We had already experienced that quite often. In the morning our train engine came after all and we continued our journey.

Around midday we were caught again unexpectedly, shortly before a small village, by another air-raid alarm. But this was only a short delay. The train stopped again after the village. Outside men's voices could be heard. We were hoping for a meal. We were suffering terribly from hunger. We had had nothing to eat for one and a half days. The guards actually went from truck to truck and let us out. They distributed goulash soup. Everything had to happen very quickly. Soon we were back inside our cages. After some time a siren sounded. When it was completely quiet again we heard the bombers flying high above us. The all-clear was given but we remained standing in the village. Some of us now began to complain about thirst. Actually we were all suffering from this affliction. In our camp the food which had been handed out contained almost no salt. The goulash soup which we had been given that day was so heavily salted and spiced that our throats and mouths seemed almost on fire even while we were eating it. The thirst was almost unbearable. It was a greater torment than our hunger. But that was not everything. We started to get stomach pains and the urge to defecate. Some simply did their business in a corner and this remained the spot for this purpose. One can imagine what a stench there was in the truck. It would have definitely been better for us not to have been given this meal. Some of us paid for this with our lives.

When it was starting to become dark we moved on again. The train moved on very slowly. We were in danger of being suffocated by the stench and the dirt. I lent on the wall and slowly sank back into a squatting position so that I was able to rest a little.

Everyone was of course terribly tired. It was now the second night without any sleep in the dark and stinking truck. We dozed on. Ranting and cursing could only be heard if somebody lost his balance when standing and fell on top of someone else. But even that night went by. You rubbed your eyes whether you had slept or not and hoped that someone would finally let us out to get some fresh air and perhaps even to get some coffee. The sun was already shining when the train actually stopped. The trucks were opened one by one. We could relieve ourselves and stretch our legs.

Everything had to happen, of course, very, very quickly. Getting back in had become very trying for us. I had to haul myself on all fours up the steps. Many others found it even harder than I did. Our hopes for coffee were in vain. After we had been locked in again the train moved on. After several stops, we arrived, tormented by unbearable hunger and thirst, in Dachau. I could have written the words on the train engine: "Here I am, back again."

The trucks were opened. We came out of the dark hole into the daylight and the fresh air. But one torment was followed by another. The terrible fear of what was to come remained. We shook at every word uttered or screamed by an SS man and collapsed inside, so to speak. Here, in the headquarters, we were much more at the mercy of the SS than in the outer camps.

We had hardly got out when we had to line up in rows of three. It did not go so badly, indeed better than I had imagined if you take our physical condition into consideration. There were a few head counts. I noticed that another man, in addition to the workmate I have already mentioned, had perished on the journey. Then came the order: "Right turn, forward march!" And we marched again through the camp gates, through which I had seen, four months previously, a group march out. I could still remember well how miserable they had all looked. Now, after four months in the concentration camp, I knew the reason why.

We looked even more wretched – one limped this way, one limped the other way, one was lop-sided, one hunchbacked. I could hardly keep up with the group. My frostbitten feet were very painful, but I made extreme efforts in order not to attract any attention. We were standing for some time, then each of us received a piece of bread and a slice of sausage. During the meal we were able to move around freely in the yard. I was one of the last to be given some bread. While I was eating it Toni Königsrainer came up to me. He had already finished eating everything up.

He asked me for a piece of bread because he had such terrible thirst. I said that bread would be no good for thirst. He asked me again for a small piece. First I looked at him and then at my bread. I felt really sorry for him but I could not give up my small piece of bread. I ate it up, thinking that he had received the same piece as I had. I can still see him today, standing sad and exhausted before me. But I think he did not even resent me for it. Shortly afterwards I saw him scooping something from a barrel in the yard. I too wanted to go over to have some of the delicious fluid. But I noticed, just in time, an SS man chasing the others away. When I came up close to the barrel, I saw that it in fact contained only dirt and mud. It would have been extremely dangerous to drink this mud. Then we were led into the shower area. There we waited for the water with an ardent yearning. When it finally came, we caught it in our hands and mouths. I will never forget this image. The shower was certainly a great blessing for us, although afterwards we had to slip into the dirty clothes which we had not changed for four weeks, and where clusters of lice and fleas were nestling in the folds.

After we had once again lined up in the yard we marched through the prison yard towards the barracks which were built on to the bunker on the left. I was already looking forward to being able to stretch out again on the bunk in the evening.

But this pleasure lasted only for a short while. With horror we saw that all the dormatories were hopelessly overcrowded. The tables which had been in every dormatory had been put into the corridor.

When we had lined up in the corridor, an SS man explained to us that this was the room where we would spend the night. Nobody was allowed to take off his clothes or shoes, not even when he was sleeping. We had, in other words, to be ready to march off at a moment's notice.

What Did They Have in Mind For Us?

Each of us asked ourselves this question again and again. Finally we were allowed to lie down on the floor. I had found a spot not far from the washroom and the toilet. I lay down on the hard floor, my head on my cap. I did not have a blanket, but fortunately it was no longer cold. My frostbitten feet were terribly painful. When the light went out I took off my shoes, although this was not permitted. It felt so good to get my sore unbandaged feet out of my shoes. Our exhaustion was so extreme that we hardly noticed the troublesome lice and other aches and pains any more. I had considered my spot to be a good one but I was cruelly mistaken. I had not been sleeping very long when I noticed a terrible pain in my foot. Someone who went to the toilet had stepped on my foot. Everyone who was staying in these barracks had to walk past me to get to the washroom. I drew my feet in and held them with my hands so that the same thing would not happen to me again. All through the night my fellow prisoners went back and forth.

In the morning I put my shoes back on again. After a shrill whistle coffee was handed out. Nowadays one would hardly call this muddy, slightly sweetish warm water, which at that time was regarded by us as a delicacy, coffee. After we had lined up in the prison yard, the SS marched with most of the prisoners out of the camp. I reported myself sick and had to go into a sideroom in which a prisoner instead of a doctor was doing the rounds. There were quite a few who had reported sick, among them also Toni Königsrainer.

During the rounds I had to lie down on a table and the doctor began to scratch away, with an instrument, at my purulent toes. I clenched my teeth in order to stop myself from screaming. Finally he sprinkled a white powder on to the raw wounds and bandaged them lightly. He also gave me a little bag with some of this powder. With that I was supposed to sprinkle the toes every day and bandage them. I left the room as if cured because I was not shouted at even once and because they really wanted to cure me. I was officially recognized as sick but had to go back to the barracks.

Around midday the siren went off and we had to go down into the water ditch behind our barracks which was roughly one and a half metres deep. The water had of course already been drained off. The sun was shining and we found it quite comfortable. We did not need to fear a bombardment of the camp. Let it thunder and crash out there so we would be set free as soon as possible.

After some time the all-clear sounded and we had to go back to the barracks. But going back had for many of us a snag, and this was the case for me too. I wanted to climb up the wall built on to the side of the ditch. I kept trying but I no longer had enough strength. Someone who has been watching this came up and helped me. After that we had to line up to get our food. There was the usual swede soup. I noticed that a different wind was blowing in the camp now. We were no longer shouted at and beaten for every little thing. We all seemed to be extremely excited.

We were Wehrmacht prisoners and as such separated from the large number of other inmates in the concentration camp. We were separated by the large building with the kitchen and washroom. It was only when we marched out of the camp or back in again that we saw the yard for the roll-call and the numerous rows of barracks. The yard for our roll-call was the so-called prison yard with the office building and the bunker in which I had spent my first days in Dachau. In this yard camp punishments, whippings and also executions by firing squad were carried out. We conscientious objectors or deserters did not wear the striped prisoners' clothes either. Instead the letters "KZ" were painted on every item of clothing. We were all sentenced to ten to fifteen years' imprisonment, followed by service on the front. So if we behaved well and were more or less able to remain standing upright, we were allowed, if need be, at the last moment, to be sent to the front. In the view of the SS this was meant to be an advantage for us compared with the real concentration camp prisoners. But all in all there was hardly any difference between us. Many of our number were shot on the spot, and some were sentenced to death and had to live in the dark cells of the bunkers in Dachau for months on end with the fear of being shot. I knew one of these condemned men who had waited for his death for sixty days, but was pardoned shortly before the liberation of the camp. He then joined our crowd and hoped with us, of course, that liberation would come soon.

The Death Transports Start to Roll

On the evening of the second day of our return from Hersbruck we received one loaf of army bread for the twelve of us. It was not the same bread as before, but a rectangular, fairly dark loaf of bread. In addition each of us received a small piece of pork fat. This evening meal was delicious, but unfortunately there was much too little of it. When it was time to go to sleep I looked for a different spot. I crept under the table and so my feet were protected. I used the shoes as a pillow. This was now my sleeping place until the liberation. The days and nights passed uneventfully. We often spent most of the day in the ditch. High above us, the bombers flew through the skies, the low-flighing aircraft much closer to the ground.

That was when I met a South Tyrolian, Alois Mantinger, a carpenter from Villnöß. He seemed to be still reasonably fit. We told each other our stories. He said to me that he had been with the police in Bolzano. His unit had almost been wiped out in Rome. He and some others were under shock, but had escaped. They no longer really knew where they should report and simply went back home. Back home the village bosses got rid of him and handed him over to the police. He was sentenced to death for deserting his unit and sent to Dachau. There he had waited for sixty days for his execution. The same thing happened to someone from Reinswald, my home village. The village bosses there got rid of him as well and handed him over to the police. He was sent to Danzig and was assigned there to a punishment battalion. Then he came to the front. He was lucky and survived. Much later I heard that he had died of dysentery, fleeing from the Russians. But nobody could officially confirm this. Alois Mantinger now helped me to get up out of the ditch every day. He was a tough guy in his early thirties. When you came across a fellow countryman this was always really encouraging. On your own you often stood on the edge of despair and lost every hope. Now more and more transports and marching columns from the outer camps were returning to Dachau. Wherever the front drew closer the camps were cleared and the prisoners were sent to the main camp. These were real death marches. For days on end they remained without food and were made to go as quickly as possible by the guards. Those who could not keep up were shot or beaten to death. As we were told later, on some of these marches only few reached their destination. It was even worse for those who were transported by train. These transports were on the move for eight to fourteen days without any food. The people had been locked in, and were unable to get out into the fresh air. Of these prisoners often only about half of them arrived in Dachau alive. The trucks with the dying and the dead presented a horrific sight. Whoever survived that would surely have to believe it was a miracle.

One day a marching column from Moosbach arrived. Although it was a long march lasting three weeks the prisoners were in relatively good condition. I was sitting in front of our barracks in the prison yard. The sun was shining, the majority of the prisoners had marched off. I was busy bandaging my sore feet.

That is when two young lads came up to me, stopped in front of me and started talking to me in German. They asked where I came from. I could see from their faces how surprised they were to meet someone from the Sarn Valley. I was of course all the more pleased to be with some more fellow countrymen again. They were two brothers, Erich and Karl Pichler from the Nesselgrube in St. Leonhard in Passeier. They had suffered the same fate as I had. Instead of joining up they had fled. Later they had given themselves up to the police, because the police had threatened to arrest their parents and all their relatives. So after some weeks in prison they had been taken to Dachau, and, from there, to the outer camp, in Moosbach. Now, after a three-week march, they had returned to Dachau. We met up quite often. Both of them were still very young, nineteen and twenty years old, very skinny and at the end of their tether. We were all afraid that they would kill all of us in the final moments before liberation. The nearer the end came, the more this worry gnawed away in our hearts.

From someone I heard that Toni Königsrainer had been taken to the sick block. I visited him. He was not so badly off and even he himself thought that he would soon be discharged. But it was the last time that I saw him. When I wanted to visit him once again a few days later, he was no longer there. I thought at first that he had been discharged, but I could not find him any more. In the final days before liberation he was not seen by anybody else either. Maybe he had fallen ill with typhoid, which had recently raged in Dachau, or he had simply perished of hunger and weakness.

The Day of Liberation

Day and night we could now hear the loud noises from the front, which was getting closer and closer. At night we saw the grenades exploding continuously. We could not get much sleep anyway.

My bones ached because I had now been lying on the hard floor for more than two weeks. I could hardly manage to turn over any more. Low-flying aircraft whizzed over us repeatedly.

One morning everyone who was somehow capable of walking was given clothes and sent to the front. Only very few of us remained behind: the two from Passeier, Erich and Karl Pichler, some Italians and myself. We did not know what this was supposed to mean. Should people without training and without weapons really simply be sent to the front? Or did they want to pick out the best of those left and finally gun down the remaining miserable creatures like us, who hardly had any chance of surviving?

The SS no longer bothered about us. You hardly saw anyone of them around. We were given our food as usual. During the day we sat around or we lent against the walls in our barracks.

With joy but also with a little fear in our hearts we waited for our liberation. There had not been a head count for two days now. These head counts were one of the most dreaded daily routines, from which many a prisoner was carried away dead.

I dozed away at night remembering the first days in the camp, thinking about the days and weeks gone by. I let what had happened pass by again in my mind. I thought that if things now went well and I escaped with my life, everything else could not be so bad. I prayed especially for peace and for the happy return of my four brothers who were fighting in the war, for my brother who had fled, for my parents and for myself. It could only be hours till liberation.

In the early morning the shooting stopped and I fell asleep. When I woke up the sun was shining in through the window. The day began fine and peacefully and made us forget all the dark and difficult days of the past. For breakfast we were even given milk coffee. Our joy and hope were increasing. It turned out to be the most beautiful, but also the most terrible day of my life.

After breakfast we strolled through the prison yard. Since no SS man appeared, we walked further in the direction of the camp gate. Nobody disturbed us on our way. We went to the property room to look for our civilian clothes. It was a large room. From the ceiling sacks were hanging, arranged precisely in alphabetical order. So I soon found my own clothes. I unpacked them; they smelt terrible. This was not surprising since they had been taken straight from my body and put into an almost air-tight sack. Browsing through my things I remembered the rosary which I had put into the torn sleeve seam to keep it safe. And I found it straight away. I wanted to put on my mountain boots again, but they had shrunk to such an extent that it was impossible to slip my swollen feet into them. I packed my civilian clothes into a suitcase which I saw lying there.

So we went with our things to the gate of the camp where we wanted to make sure that we were free. The gate was open. Of course we did not hesitate for long and walked out without knowing what we actually wanted to do. We now came to the SS camp which before had been completely out of bounds for us. We approached the SS kitchen in the hope of finding something edible. Unfortunately our hope was in vain. All the pots were empty; we did not even find a piece of bread. We went out again into the yard and were now almost certain that we were really free. We could have jumped in the air for joy.

I felt like a little child that is still uncertain on its feet and falls over easily. Because I was so weak I could not jump in the air but I was ready for any fun. From this moment on I forgot everything that had happened before. One must have experienced what we had gone through in order to be able to understand what freedom meant for us at this moment.

We strolled around in the SS area, looked into various barracks, but what we were actually looking for, something edible – we did not find. Now and then we saw an SS man looking out of a window of the barracks, but no one bothered about us. We went into the clothes store and browsed around there for a while. Then we heard a few shots. When we looked cautiously out of the window, we saw an SS man rolling on the ground behind the barracks, then jumping up and disappearing. Opposite two Americans were creeping through the pine wood, from one tree to another, towards us. They disappeared behind the SS barracks and we continued browsing in the store. We packed up some things in order to take them home with us. And then somebody had the idea of exchanging our lice-infested shirts with the ones we had found here. No sooner said than done. We had been wearing these dirty shirts which were full of insects for nearly two months. While we were fiddling around, the door was suddenly pulled open and in walked two Americans with machine guns at the ready. We smiled at them; after all they were our liberators. One of them ordered us to go with him. We wanted to take the things we had packed with us but he indicated to us that we could get them later. We were only to go with them for a short while. So we simply followed them as we were, without our jackets, only with our shoes, trousers and with the new clean shirts. The sun was shining. It was beautiful spring weather.

We trudged with the men past several barracks and buildings and came to a big gate. Inside in the yard a number of SS men who had been shot were lying. One of them was still alive and wanted to sit up. But he was finally gunned down with a few shots. As we went past we thought to ourselves that they had deserved it, that this was their just punishment.

We were ordered to stand still and were positioned not far from the SS men, with our faces to the wall. We had to hold our hands together over our heads. Then a chill went down my spine. They had tracked us down, not in the prisoners' camp, but in the SS camp in which they had previously captured the SS men and had then shot them in the yard. Moreover several of us were wearing the new SS shirts which we had previously exchanged for our own shirts. So it was possible that we had been mistaken for SS men and made to stand against the wall.

I felt hot one moment and cold the next. I was already imagining how the men behind us were aiming their guns at us. I would probably take only a few seconds until they gunned us down as well. I prayed. I really did not want to die now.

In the morning we had experienced great joy over gaining our freedom and the hope of a rapid homecoming – and now in the afternoon the fear of being shot. This was simply too much all at once. I cried, prayed, and all sort of thoughts went through my mind. There could be a bang at any moment. The fear which I felt then will never be forgotten. Beside me stood the two men from Passeier, Erich and Karl Pichler, and some Italians. I do not know how long we stood there. At any rate it seemed to me to go on forever. Behind us we heard voices. Then we were allowed to take our hands down and turn round. I saw a few American officers and some soldiers with machine guns in their hands. Surely they had just been discussing our fate and finally came to the conclusion that we were not SS people, but prisoners who had escaped from the camp too soon. They drove us out of the SS camp and we trudged along the road. I felt as if I had been beaten and was trembling all over, because I could not yet believe that we had escaped with our lives. Outside the camp we were led into a fairly large building where we met several captive soldiers. The soldiers, who still had rucksacks, had to unpack everything. They had to hand over all the food, the tins and the bread. I was standing beside a soldier and saw a large loaf of bread in his rucksack. I could not stop looking at it because I felt so terribly hungry and asked the soldier for a piece. He hesitated for some time but because I did not give up he gave me a small piece. Then we had to go through a check point and I saw that they took away the whole loaf from the soldier. The guard looked at me with astonishment because I had neither a coat nor a cap nor a jacket, and probably he was struck by my pale, emaciated face. We had to go into a large building. The place looked like a theatre auditorium without benches and chairs. At the front there was a big wooden stage. There may have been about a hundred to a hundred and fifty prisoners there. We prisoners of the concentration camp had been simply put with the captive soldiers.

It was nearly evening and we all were hungry, but they told us that we would get the food which they had taken from the soldiers only the following midday. Many grumbled and cursed, but it did not help. We camp prisoners quite often had to go without food for two to three days and had not died as a consequence.

When I realized that there would be no evening meal I looked around for a place to lie down. I went on to the wooden stage, took off my shoes and lay down against the wall. I was very tired and despondent and wanted to sleep.

But now my sore feet made themselves felt and all my bones were aching. That day I did not even have a jacket or a coat with me but only a shirt and trousers. I put my shoes under my head and pushed my feet against the wall so that nobody could step on them. In spite of my tiredness I could not get to sleep so quickly. The day had been too unsettling: in the morning the infinitely great joy of being free, and in the afternoon the terrible shock of being put up against the wall. In our SS shirts the Americans had probably only recognized us as prisoners of the concentration camp because we behaved towards them in a particularly cheerful way. Our pitiful appearance had probably made the Americans think again.

Because we were wearing a variety of different clothes, we had not been sent to the camp but to the captive soldiers. There was an unsettled and mixed atmosphere in the room. Some were happy to have escaped unharmed from the front, others complained about their captivity. I was happy to have escaped with my life once again. For me the last hours had been, so to speak, the last station of my ordeal in the concentration camp.

Not far away from us the fierce fighting continued. There was a continuous crashing and thundering noise. When it became dark we could see the flashing lights of the bullets. It lasted another three days until all was quiet. I felt somehow freed from the reign of terror, but was still – and once again – a prisoner, and my time of suffering was to continue.

The night went by with a lot of anxiety about the days to come. One should not – as the morning had shown – celebrate too soon.

The following day the weather was wonderful once again. The sun shone in through the window and cheered us up a little. But one pain gnawed away at all of us: a tremendous hunger. The soldiers who might have eaten enough the day before complained a lot. We, however, who had been starving for months and were only skin and bone accepted our fate. More and more new prisoners were added to our number. Midday was approaching and we were all waiting intently for the meal that had been promised. But instead they told us we would get something to eat the following day. Yet another day without food! We cursed and swore about the poor organization. I fully accepted my lot; in the concentration camp we had not been allowed to protest and here it was pointless anyway. I prayed again and again and particularly when the situation seemed to me to be desperate I gained new hope through prayer.

Six Days of Starvation

I sat there leaning on the wall and busied myself with my sore toes. On one foot they had healed a little since the treatment, but the condition of the toes on the other foot looked bad. I could of course bandage them again, but that was no use because I had neither ointment nor anything else to put on them. I turned the bandage around or moved it further, until after some time it was completely covered with pus and blood. There was no water to wash them; the shoes were full of dirt because my feet sometimes bled while I was walking. I had a lot of trouble slipping, without socks, into my hard, dirty shoes.

I lent against the wall, half asleep, half awake. We heard a crashing and thundering noise from the front. A fierce battle was taking place near Munich; the Germans still did not want to give up. An older man was standing in a brown uniform beside me. He had probably been watching me for quite some time and had seen my miserable situation. He shook my shoulder and bent down towards me in order to ask me whether I really had no jacket, coat and blanket. I said I did not, and turned away from him because, in my exhaustion, I did not want to be disturbed.

I crouched there, leaning with my back against the wall, my legs tucked up, my arms around my knees and my head bent forward. I was hoping to be able to sleep in this position. But the man did not leave me in peace. He shook me again and I looked up to him in distress. He was holding a coat for me and said he would give it to me; he had another one for himself. I took the coat gratefully, and was surprised and pleased that somebody had taken pity on me. Without this coat I would definitely not have survived the following days. The man left me, disappeared among the prisoners and I never saw him again. I put the coat over my shoulders and dozed away.

Hour after hour went by, more and more prisoners were brought in and it now became quite cramped in the room. This night was a bit quieter. The front had moved away a bit and no long disturbed us. I had put on my coat. It was so big that I could wrap it twice around myself, and I slept relatively well.

In the morning we rubbed our eyes a bit because there was nothing to wash with. The weather was cloudy and overcast, and the atmosphere in our room was dull and downcast as well. We were greatly tormented by hunger. Food was the only thing we all still talked about and we waited for the promised midday meal. Many people grumbled and complained again. I prayed a little instead and my hope was renewed.

While we were waiting longingly for the food we were shocked to receive the order to pack everything ready to march off.

I did not have anything to pack, but was still the last one to go out through the gate. There were about three hundred prisoners. For many of us it was the third day without food.

We marched for some time along a road. I had great difficulty in keeping up. My strength slowly disappeared, which was no surprise, and my feet were sore. The Americans kept driving us on. After a while we came to a meadow somewhere between Dachau and Munich on which hundreds of prisoners were already standing, and more and more joined them. Around the meadow there was tangled wire in the form of a circle. Machine guns were positioned in order to prevent people from fleeing.

It began to rain a little and it was rather cool. Among the newcomers we looked for people we knew and tried to beg for a piece of bread.

The evening came. Some pitched a tent and crawled inside. We saw many groups of people who were holding tent canvas over their heads to protect themselves from the rain. I realized now how valuable the coat I had been given was. Without it I would definitely have died. We trudged slowly around in the camp, in order not to die of cold.

We were surrounded by floodlights, but some people tried to escape. Late at night we heard machine gun fire. Prisoners had cut through the wire circuit in a somewhat darker corner and a large number of them had escaped. When the American guards saw this they shot at those who were fleeing. Some of them managed to escape, others were wounded and some were also killed. I could not even think of escaping; I was far too weak for that.

In the early morning it began to snow. The ground was cold and wet. We could neither lie down nor sit down. I was very tired and sometimes squatted. So I sat for a time on my heels until I fell asleep, lost my balance and fell over. I think

I sometimes slept, from sheer tiredeness, for minutes on end while still standing.

As usual I thought about food. We could have really done with warm tea or coffee. But it was hopeless. We kept being put off until the next day. And this was the fourth day on which we had been given nothing to eat. It was becoming worse than in the concentration camp, apart from the fear of being wiped out. In addition there was the bad weather. The coat which had become wet and heavy because of the rain, was becoming a burden to me. And yet I needed it to protect me from the cold and rain.

It rained more or less the whole day. Towards evening it started to snow slightly again. In the camp the mood was becoming more and more agitated, and again and again some tried to break out in the darkness. However you perished, it made no difference. Some might have managed to escape but there were always the wounded and dead left behind because the Americans simply shot into the crowd. Most of us were soaked through to the skin and we were all tormented by an indescribable hunger.

I was afraid of the night. I could not lie down. The ground was covered with puddles and the earth had been trampled to mud by the large number of prisoners. "How will I survive this night? Will I survive it at all? Perhaps I will be lying in the morning, huddled up somewhere, dead on the ground."

These thoughts kept going through my head. Then I forced myself again to hang on, and I recalled the consoling words of the head of the camp in Hersbruck who had encouraged me to hang on in order to be able to return to beautiful South Tyrol and to my dear ones at home. While I was praying for a happy return home a few tears rolled down my face. I let them flow freely because I was not ashamed to cry in my misery.

At night I slept a bit in a squatting position but I had to walk around again and again to warm myself up.

Right into the late morning of the following day we were hoping for tea or coffee. Then our hope disappeared. We heard that water was available somewhere in the camp. But there was so much pushing and shoving that only the stronger prisoners got to the water. People like me would have been trampled to death.

It had stopped raining and snowing, but it was still misty and fairly cool. It was the fifth day without food and I no longer thought we would get any. I slowly lost the courage and strength to continue living. My friends who had always encouraged me were somewhere in the crowd. I gave up, was tired and only wanted to continue sleeping. Then there were the thoughts of my dear ones at home, but they were too fleeting to give me hope. I had put everything in order with the Lord God, I thought. I surrendered myself entirely to his will.

I slowly sank down on to the wet and dirty ground and I thought I would fall asleep and never wake up again and my indescribable misery would come to an end.

I had been preoccupied for some time with these thoughts when somebody shook me by the shoulder and said to me: "Hey, Sarner*, get up!" It was the Pichler brothers from

---

* Translators' footnote: a Sarner is man from the Sarn Valley

133

Passeier who had happened to see me lying there and had immediately recognized me. They said I should pull myself together and get up because I would perish here on the ground. They would not let us starve to death.

I did not believe them, but the two of them did not give up and helped me to get up. They said that we would have to hang on for only a short time in order to get back home.

The word "homecoming" gave me hope again and I trusted my comrades once again. They no longer let me out of their sight, otherwise I would perhaps have given up once again. My comrades were for me at this moment real guardian angels. My strength would no longer have been sufficient. I had always believed in help through prayer and so I hoped once again, through the prayers of my dear ones at home and our own prayers, and with the help of my comrades, to get away from here.

The weather had improved and from time to time the sun even shone. This did not help to cheer us up either. The ground soon dried up a little so that we could sit or lie down. That evening we still had not been given any food, but the people in charge assured us that it would definitely happen the following day.

The night was cool; the prisoners stood together in groups. Some spread out the tarpaulin on the ground and lay down on it, others squatted back to back to support each other. I simply lay down with my coat on the ground and turned the collar up to avoid lying with my head on the bare ground. I soon fell asleep but kept waking up. Now I was frightened that I would never wake up again. The brothers from Passeier remained sitting or standing close to me. So this night went by as well. It became light early and it looked like it would be a nice day. Our thoughts were once again about food.

Food

In the late afternoon there was great jubilation. We watched as the Americans unloaded from big lorries a lot of cardboard boxes with tinned food in several places outside our camp. But several hours went by until they were distributed. Imagine the thrill of anticipation! For many it was the sixth day without food. We all looked at the boxes and were eating the food in our imagination.

I had only one worry: it was always the strongest who pushed their way forward and I thought the same thing could happen to me as had happened when I tried to get water, when I did not dare to do the same as the others so as not to be trampled to death. But in this case it was done fairly, thank God. Many prisoners were standing in long queues behind each box, and then it started. Each one of us had to go past the distribution point and while he was running two tins of food were thrown to him by two Americans. Everything went rather quickly, but I was standing right at the back and had to wait a long time until it was my turn. I looked very anxiously at the distribution point because I was afraid that there would not be enough. Finally it was my turn. I could not run, but pulled myself together to pass by quickly and catch the tins that were thrown to me. They were very small tins; one was heavy, the other very light.

I looked for a spot and sat down in a cross-legged position. When I opened the tins I heard and saw nothing around me any more. One tin contained green beans in oil, the other three biscuits, a small piece of chocolate and four sweets. Before I started eating I broke out in tears. I had not seen delicacies like this for a long time. After months of starvation and the last six days without food and without water, I began to eat. Tears kept on running down my face and I swallowed many a tear. According to a wise saying, you have to eat bread mixed with tears once in your life in order to be able to appreciate its true value. I would certainly not wish this on anybody, but some people actually could have a bit more respect for bread.

I will never forget this meal, and some other meals, for the rest of my life, even though it was much too meagre. I felt new hope. At this moment I forgot all the sad things that had happened before and thanked God that he had let me survive these hard days.

I sat there for a long time and then started to become interested again in what was happening around me. Not very far from me I saw my comrades from Passeier and it was consoling not to be alone. I think that they had watched me before during my meal and did not want to disturb me. When they saw that I was looking around in search of somebody, they came up to me. We talked for a while about the good meal and thought that things would start to get better again. They also knew that the following day they would start transferring us to another camp. That night I slept relatively well. I felt a bit cold because my clothes were still a little wet due to the bad weather the previous day. I looked forward to the sun the following day.

And indeed they started to drive the prisoners off in lorries. I had the impression that the prisoners were sorted according to their nationality. By midday many prisoners had already been taken away.

I saw that some people outside the camp were going to a small hut and I immediately thought that there must be some food there. Some delicious porridge was being distributed. After a short time it was my turn and somebody lent me his bowl and spoon. I saw a large pot in front of me – still half full of porridge. I though I could have eaten it all up on my own. I received quite some portion. It tasted superb. The porridge was sweet and fairly thick, almost like puree. It was just the right thing for us: easily digestible but nonetheless nourishing.

I was among the last to be taken away. A few comrades pulled me on to the lorry where we were herded so closely together that you could not have fallen over. We were then unloaded again somewhere else, were added to the other prisoners, had to move on again and thus came via Heilbronn to the French border. There we met the other comrades from the concentration camp again who were to be sent on the 25th of April to the front. They said that they did not get far. They had received clothes but no weapons. Some of them had fled, for instance Luis Mantinger from Villnöß and probably also my former Italian work colleague, Giovanni Filz from Trentino, of whom I had not heard anything.

The camps in which we were held – in the open air – were always just fields fenced in with wire. We were exposed to all weathers, and those of us who were weak suffered greatly. Later I often remembered these times when I went up the mountain in spring or summer in bad weather and saw the animals just standing there without any cover. I, and some of the others, developed a new ailment. My feet, and also my head, particularly the area around my eyes, became so swollen that I could hardly see the following morning. I remembered a colleague in the Hersbruck camp whose body was also swollen for some time and who had then died. For this reason I was very frightened that this could be a warning sign of imminent death. I looked terrible and wanted to conceal my face from the others.

When I was in this condition a comrade told me he had met another man from the Sarn Valley. I was eager to find out whether I knew him. Then I remembered my appearance and I was afraid that he would not recognize me and not accept me as a fellow countryman. When I met him I saw that he was not somebody I knew, a somewhat older man. We did not know each other but it turned out in the course of the conversation that he knew my parents and some of my brothers. He said he was the "Strecker Martl" (Martin Schwitzer) from Pens and that he would take care of me. From then on Martl was my great guardian and he helped me wherever he could. But also the brothers from Passeier kept inquiring about how I was. They were not much stronger than I was. But because they were always together they could console and encourage each other. Had this not been the case they would have been in the same situation as I had been some days previously, one of them once said. So I was happy to have found somebody who took care of me and was himself more or less strong enough.

My new comrade and I told each other, bit by bit, what we had experienced. We soon discovered that we had the same opinions about Hitler. He too had been persecuted as an anti-Nazi, had been put in prison and finally sent to the front with a punishment batallion, where he had experienced terrible things, but had survived without being wounded. He was a deeply religious person. We often prayed together, and not at all secretly or quietly. He had a strong voice. We were ridiculed or made fun of by many, but that did not bother us, especially not Martl. If somebody offended him he would rebuke him with a few serious words, so that the latter preferred to move off again. With his thirty-nine years and his serious face he radiated authority so that he was actually rarely pestered. I was pleased about that and felt stronger myself.

Everytime we moved to another camp we were "frisked". This was a kind of check when you had to go past the American soldiers and put down on the ground in front of them everything that was in your trouser pockets or in your jacket. It was then often the case that what had been put down by one person was picked up again by the next person in an unobserved moment. I had nothing to hand over, so I looked to see if there was something I could take. This was how I once took a valuable pocket knife, which was stolen from me a short time afterwards. On another occasion I managed to take a nice leather purse, which however was empty. I took it home with me although I was "frisked" before each new camp.

During one camp control the prisoners had to line up. Many of us were so weak that our first attempt to get up from the ground was not successful. When they came to check us, not all of us were on our feet. One of them asked what was wrong with us. One prisoner who was able to speak a little English said that we were so weak because of lack of food that we could not get up. From then on we were allowed to remain lying down when they came to do their checks.

When we were once again transferred to another camp and we were standing and lying in the open air, they said that the prisoners had to register for an examination in the large tent next to the camp. So Martl dragged me there once again. In the tent there were about ten doctors, prisoners as well, standing in a row, some metres away from each other. They were supposed to examine us, probably as a prophylactic measure against infectious diseases. We were deloused by having our clothes dusted down with large quantities of powder. We had to take everything off and I had to keep holding on to Martl in order not to fall over. When it was my turn I went up to the doctor. He looked at me from head to toe, shook his head, looked again and again and then went over to the other doctors. They all came over to me and looked with astonishment at my wretched body. They kept shaking their heads and wondered how a human being could survive in this condition.

In another camp the kitchen was situated in the camp itself and separated from us by tangled wire. I still remember well that waste of different kinds from the kitchen was thrown away. Usually it was only coffee grounds; we grabbed handfulls of it in order to chew on it for some time. Those who got hold of raw potato peelings were better off. All the weeds that could be reached near the fence around the camp, particularly dandelion or other green leaves, were eaten up immediately. Our hunger was so great that the possibility of being poisoned did not even occur to anyone.

One day we were told that we would be sent to France to a large prison camp. People then started to moan; some did not believe it, some swore and said that they should let us go home. All this lamentation did not help and finally the day arrived. It may have been towards the end of May. We were not far away from the border. We had to pack everything early in the morning but after that things went rather slowly. We were given coffee and then were loaded on to lorries. It was late morning before we drove off. The weather was foggy and dull, so that we could not see much of the countryside. I did not notice the border at all. After forty-five hours' travelling we stopped. Unloading had to be done very quickly again. The empty lorries drove off and only some jeeps with a lot of guards remained behind. They put us in marching order, in rows of four. Martl and I were roughly in the middle of the column. At the front a jeep drove forward slowly, but still too fast for us to march. We went through a forest and up a fairly steep road. I had problems keeping up from the beginning and others kept overtaking me. Behind us we could hear screaming and a shot from time to time. I told Martl that I would soon be finished but he encouraged me and let me hold on to his coat. He kept telling me that it would alright and I gave everything I could. Someone next to me said that he had seen how someone who could not keep up was shot down, and fell into the ditch. This was a big blow for me because I was about to give up anyway. We were already the last ones in the marching column and even a few steps behind the others. There were shouts from behind me but I did not understand a word. Suddenly somebody kicked me so that I was thrown a few metres forward. Martl helped me up again. My bones were still aching even weeks later. Martl took me by the hand and pulled me behind him. I kept thinking that I could not go on, I cried like a child and was completely finished. Then I thought again that I did not want to end up in the ditch, but to live and get home. But I would not be able to keep going much longer. Many a time I felt near the end of my life. But I had a good guardian angel and with his help and with the help of all the saints whom I kept calling upon in this indescribable misery I managed it this time as well.

After having marched in such misery along the uphill road, we came out of the wood and the road became even, so that it was easier for me to keep up. Immediately we then saw the large camp with its many big tents. I was pleased and hoped to get into one of these tents so as not be exposed to the open air and to all weathers. We marched into the camp. To the left and to the right of the wide road there were big tents, all of which were open so you could look inside. We stopped and were assigned to different tents. I was sent to the tent for the sick. Down the middle of the tent there was a passageway which was about seventy centimetres wide and marked off on both sides with wooden boards. There were beds of straw on both sides. Each of us was given two blankets. It felt as if things would get much better.

We were given our food, that is two tins, and we started eating. Each of us was sitting on his spot. There may have been twenty-four men in our tent. There was quite a lot of room, and we were actually able to move around. Those who were fit and well, on the other hand, had to share a space with fifty others in a tent. Behind our tent there was a large communal toilet. When we had eaten our rations we prepared our beds. I spread one blanket underneath, put a bundle of straw under my head and covered myself with the other blanket. All I wanted to do then was sleep. This day was probably for me the most difficult day; physically and mentally I was completely finished. My comrades often told me later that they had no longer believed that I would manage to go on. But with their help I was able to persevere and so I am right to call them my saviours.

My young life was totally ruined by these six months, during five of which we were tortured almost to death by hunger, disease and hard work in the hell of the concentration camp, and after which we were kept prisoner by the Americans for a further month, by the death wall, by every possible tribulation in the various camps and by the march to this place, which had driven me almost to desperation. I will probably have to suffer from this physically and mentally for the rest of my life.

In the Prison Camp in France

This day put an end to my suffering. In this new prison camp a totally new life started for us – after months of not being treated as human beings. In the tent we could now lie on straw and were no longer exposed to bad weather. I slept well in the tent in this first night. Only from time to time did I wake up with a fright. In the morning they brought us coffee to the tent without our having to get up. It was milk coffee but we were not given any bread. Two male nurses served us. They took our temperature, and, like several others, I had thirty-eight degrees. They also treated my sore feet. At midday we had oatmeal soup with apricots and afterwards we were able to sleep again and recover from the agonies we had been through. Later in the afternoon they brought us bread. It was rectangular, ten-centimetres-thick white bread, whiter than we had ever seen before. We all looked at it with surprise and could hardly wait for it to be distributed. Four men had to share a loaf, but for those who were ill like us it was only two who had to share. We received a piece of chocolate or a little jam to go with it. The food was good, but of course there was still too little of it. Probably it was better this way. Later our temperature was taken again and we discussed and talked politics. Most of all we were delighted with the humanity with which we were treated here. We had new hopes of getting home.

In the camp it soon became known that some former prisoners from the concentration camp were in the sick tent and were in a very bad condition. This was always known to the kitchen staff. I think it was Martl who advocated that we should be allowed to get a pot full of oat meal soup every day, in addition to the usual rations. I received a four-litre tin which had contained dried apricots. The cook filled my tin almost up to the brim with soup. I thanked him with tears in my eyes and walked back to the tent as quickly as my shaky legs could carry me. On the way I kept looking into the tin and could hardly wait till I could eat. In one hand I was already holding the broken spoon without a handle, which I had once found somewhere. I sat down in a cross-legged position on my straw bed and began to eat. I could eat for a long time. I was not aware of what was going on around me. When I could not get any more out with the spoon, I wiped everything clean with my finger because I could not get enough of it. I could probably have eaten another tin full of soup. There was a lot of water in it and for that reason the soup was easily digestible. And so days and weeks went by with nothing changing in the camp.

I recovered only very slowly. After three weeks in the sick tent I still had a temperature. Nothing was done about this apart from letting me lie day and night. Time and rest were the only things which I had enough of. I wondered then what things would be like at home, how the end of the war had been. I had not heard anything further from home since November, and I wondered how things had gone for my brother who had also fled, whether he had had to give himself up, whether my parents had been arrested because of him, whether my four brothers who had been fighting in the war, were all still alive or whether perhaps one or other of them had died in the war. I spent most of my time preoccupied with these thoughts.

Later, when I had recovered a little and the weather was good, I walked around in the camp quite often. In this way I met another two men from the Sarn Valley: "Irscher Luis" and Josef Reichsigl (nicknamed "Erschbaum Sepp"), whom I knew from home.

In the camp all sorts of things were made using various handicrafts; from the metal of the cans tobacco tins or similar things were made. Because I could do a little engraving I inscribed my name on my food tin and decorated it with flowers. The others saw this and I had to do the same for some of them. In this way, for three or four hours of work, I was able to earn a few mouthfuls of bread, for which some people envied me. One can hardly imagine nowadays how highly we valued bread at that time. It was divided up and weighed exactly with improvised scales; when one piece was bigger than another, a bit was cut off. The smallest crumbs were eaten up from the ground with hardly a second thought.

It will have become obvious by now that I keep talking about hunger and eating, but this really was a great affliction. Because of our constant hunger over months, for some even over years, we had simply become childish. We spoke about food like children and begged each other for a piece of bread or a spoon of soup. It did not make any difference whether you were seventeen- or eighteen-years-old, or were more mature and forty or fifty years-old. From time to time we heard various rumours, on one occasion that they would send us to a prison camp in Italy, on another that we would soon be allowed to go home. We no longer actually believed in such talk, but some people obviously enjoyed spreading new rumours in the camp on a daily basis.

Martl and I met almost every day, particularly when the weather was good, to recite the evening rosary prayers. For this we sat at the edge of the campsite, on the slope before the ring fence. The prisoners strolled around in the camp in the evening. First there were only the two of us who prayed; as time went on more and more joined in and we were pleased about that, particularly Martl. His strong voice became louder and louder, so that he could be heard in the wider vicinity. Often we sat or stood around for a long time and watched the beautiful sunset. That was wonderful. The sun became darker and darker until it disappeared as a red ball, and immediately afterwards it became dark.

Once an Italian priest came to our camp and a celebration was prepared. They set up an altar and there was also the opportunity for confession. I went for a walk with the priest, a bit away from the others, and received the sacrament of penance. Although he only spoke Italian we understood each other well because I had a lot to do with a large number of Italians in the concentration camp. It was a great joy to be open about being a Christian in public again, something which had been forbidden in the camp under threat of severe punishment. The following day there was a celebratory service. A fairly big crowd of prisoners formed the choir, which sang moving prison songs. The priest encouraged us in his sermon to make sacrifices and to persevere. He could ensure us that we would soon return home to our loved ones. So we celebrated the holy mass with great devotion as a thanksgiving for surviving many hard hours and as a request for a happy homecoming. I think that everyone, with only a few exceptions, took part, including those of us who were from South Tyrol. For we had declared ourselves to be Italians when we had been asked about our nationality. I did not have any reservations about this. They had persecuted and intended to kill me as an Italian citizen and so I happily returned to my native land as such.

About a week later, it may have been in the first days of August, the names of the Italian prisoners were registered and they said that a commission would come from Italy to check everything and take us home. We were happy to be finally going home again. Some South Tyrolians had changed their minds and declared themselves to be Austrians. But that only delayed their homecoming. As I learned later they had to go to work for another six months, which actually meant in a work camp. And after that, when they wanted to return to their South Tyrolian homeland, they had to declare themselves again to be Italian citizens or to apply for Italian citizenship.

And so the days went by in joyful hope.

In this camp I had recovered over time to the extent that I could walk around more often. It was only getting up which still caused me difficulty. I then became dizzy and had to hold on to something.

One afternoon I went to the kitchen as usual to get the soup which we former prisoners were given. The kitchen was separated from the camp by a wire fence. When I came to the opening where a prisoner always stood on guard, he stopped me and said that he was not allowed to let anyone through who was not fully dressed. As usual I had only a shirt and a short pair of pants, which up to this point had not bothered anybody.

After a short exchange of words I went straight past him into the kitchen and got my soup as always. When I came past the guard on my way back he told me very angrily that he would report it to the boss. I did not think about this much, went into my tent, ate the soup with enjoyment and told my comrades what had happened to me. They said he was probably envious of me.

The following morning two men came from the security force which was established within the camp and asked for Franz Thaler, who had disobeyed the guard at the kitchen gate the previous day. I reported and was asked why I had done this. I explained that nobody before had been bothered about my clothes. I had thought that he wanted to tease me. The two men said that I should not have disobeyed the guard and I would therefore have to spend three days in detention.

The place of detention was located at the end of the campsite and was a tent which was open on the front side. In the middle there was a small shaky table and a few chairs on the bare ground. The tent was surrounded by tangled wire, and there was a narrow gate in the corner, closed with a lock. I had gone past there every day and admit that I had sometimes looked with contempt at the men who were being punished in there for theft or for the brawl which had ensued. Now I had to go in there myself. I was a prisoner twice over and for that I had to thank a South Tyrolian, whose name I do not want to mention although I remember him well. I can still picture the "young whippersnapper" which he then was, very well. Probably he was one of those Tyrolians who, whenever possible, preferred power to our highly-esteemed sense of comradeship.

For me it was a setback; I felt myself excluded from the community.

At that time it did not take much to make me feel sad. The mental pain was usually worse than the physical pain. It did not take long until my true comrades came to the detention tent and comforted me. Actually I was not really badly off; I got just as much food, or rather just as little food, as outside the detention tent. The only things I could not do were walk around freely in the camp and lie down during the day. At night we were allowed to return to our tent.

In the afternoon of the second day someone collected us and we were once again registered by an Italian commission. I had to return once more to the detention tent, but nothing could make me sad anymore because it was only a few days until our journey home. I was discharged from the sick tent because of my "crime" but nonetheless assigned to the sick transport. They said that the sick would be the first to leave. There was great joy, and everyone spoke only about going home.

On the third day I was discharged from detention and taken to another tent. There was so little space there that we all had to lie on our sides in order to have room. If you had to go to the toilet it was necessary to make a good mental note of your spot in order to be able to squeeze in again afterwards. It actually looked good: we were squeezed into the space like sardines in a tin. Fortunately I had to sleep there for only two nights.

The Journey Home

In the afternoon of the 14th of August 1945 those who belonged to the sick transport had to pack everything and prepare to march off. It was only the sick who no longer needed to remain lying and no longer needed care. The only things we actually had to pack were our spoons and our food canisters, as well as the small tins of food which we were given as provisions for the march. We were taken by lorry to the train. The train was already standing there. We were counted and had to get in. To our great surprise it was not a cattle truck anymore, but a normal passenger train, third-class. We still thought that we were being held under guard, but felt that we were being treated as human beings.

In the evening we set off and were bound for home. Our joy was great. The train rattled along without any hurry. It did not seem to be in a rush to take us home. I dozed away but could not sleep. However the night went past quickly. Daybreak came early and soon the sun was shining through the windows. It was the 15th of August, the day of the Assumption of Mary, and I thought that we would celebrate that feast day at home. In my thoughts I was celebrating as well, and I thanked the Mother of God for the protection and the comfort which I had received from her, and promised – if it was at all possible – to go on a pilgrimage once a year to Maria Trens. We had long since eaten up our provisions for the march and hunger increasingly made itself felt. Finally the train stopped in a small village – still in France – and after some time they brought us tea and pieces of bread. After we had eaten we were allowed to get out and to walk around freely within earshot.

I walked with a few comrades along a meadow track and again and again, first one of us, then another, looked back because we thought there must be a guard following us, with his gun at the ready. We just could not believe that for once we did not have barbed wire around us, and that we were allowed to simply walk around freely among the field flowers.

Not far away we saw a small chapel with a few houses, and the only thing that was missing to make the picture complete was the mountains in the background. For me there was a sense of genuinely pleasant anticipation. I will never forget the first day in freedom, under the blue sky, among the field flowers, just as I will never forget many a hard day in the concentration camp or in captivity, when I stood on the ground which had been trampled to death and looked longingly through the barbed wire into the world of freedom.

After a few hours we had to get in again and the journey continued towards Switzerland. In the train we were not under surveillance by guards. Our escorts turned out to be merely guides who were supposed to take us home.

The following day the weather was once again splendid. I had not slept long and when the sun was shining I felt really alive. It was wonderful to travel through this landscape with beautiful little houses which had beautiful flowers on their balconies and with the mountains all around, which

I, as a Tyrolian, had been missing for a long time. Around midday we reached a larger village in which they gave us breakfast. Some men handed out bread, biscuits and butter and poured us coffee. They went from compartment to compartment and said they hoped we would have a good meal and above all a happy return home. This was our first encounter with civilians for almost a year.

After we had been there for some time the train moved on. It was almost too slow for us. Night came and we dozed away. After we had passed through a long tunnel we were told that we were now in Italy.

At dawn the train stopped. We were hoping in vain to get breakfast but then we went on. Around midday we arrived in Novara. After having waited in the train at the station we had to get out. We walked through the station out on to the street where we met a lot of women and children. They all spoke Italian and greeted us in a friendly way. We went through the streets towards some run-down barracks. We had to go into a large room on the ground floor. The room was more like a car garage than a place for people to stay. The floor was dirty and in one corner there was a pile of straw on which blankets were lying around all over the place. Probably this place had been used as prisoners' quarters before us. We received a good portion of pasta asciutta, which we were very pleased about. This time we were kept more under guard, this time by Italians. Whenever we German speakers spoke in our mother tongue we were looked at suspiciously. This was not surprising because the Italians had suffered unspeakably at the hands of the Germans. They of course did not know that we, just like them, had been persecuted by the Germans. And so they probably felt hatred rising up inside whenever they heard German being spoken. We were not allowed to leave the room and became bored. We wanted to go home. Instead a guard told us that we would be taken still further south to a prison camp. This made us feel sad, although we could not really believe it because they had promised to set us free and let us return home. The evening came and we had to make due with the dirty pile of straw as a place to lie down. They gave us blankets; we spread them out and lay down. What we had feared, namely ending up in a nest of lice, did not come true. I slept into the morning. We received coffee and bread and discussed this and that afterwards. The pessimists said we would have to wait around a long time in camps; others thought that we would definitely soon be home. I shared the opinion of the second group. They would not really keep their own people as prisoners. At midday we again received a large portion of pasta asciutta and our hunger was stilled. It was rather warm and we preferred to stay in the shade. Some lay down on the straw in order to let the time pass more quickly by taking a nap.

In the late afternoon several men wearing civilian clothes arrived and handed out provisional discharge documents. This was how we learned we would soon be returning home. In the evening each of us received a piece of bread, biscuits and tea. We waited impatiently to continue our journey and when it became dark we lay down again on the pile of straw to sleep.

On the following morning – on the 18th of August – we hoped we would get away soon after breakfast. And indeed we had to get ourselves ready to march to the station and to get into a normal carriage. There were some compartments reserved for us. The train soon moved off. It stopped briefly in Milan and some people got out because they had to continue their journey in a different direction. We said good-bye to our Italian colleagues with friendly words and "Have a safe journey home". The train went on in the direction of Verona.

We all had to get off there. We were given supplies for the march and said good-bye once again to many comrades. There were only ten to twelve men left who were travelling to Trentino.

We were now completely free and had to look after ourselves for the remainder of the journey. We inquired at the station about a train to Bolzano, but it did not look good. Because the wait until evening was too long for us and we heard that an engine without any carriages was travelling to Trentino, we kept pleading until they took us with them. We were allowed to hang on to the outside of the engine. It was fairly warm; we were really sweating. The steam engine was fired by coal and sometimes the wind carried the smoke into our faces so that we nearly choked.

When we arrived in Trentino we were black as coal. The smoke had covered our sweat-covered faces like soot. We went to a fountain to wash our hands and faces, but with cold water and without any soap we did not manage to remove the dirt. Here as well some comrades stayed behind. Those of us who were left did not want to waste much time and wanted to move on immediately. But how? There was no train. We went on to the road and a lorry soon came. We stopped it and were allowed to get in.

It was shortly before nine o'clock in the evening when we reached the station in Bolzano. We expressed our sincere thanks to the driver and said good-bye. I wanted to hurry on in order perhaps to catch somebody with a car or some sort of vehicle in the Rößl-Wirt in Bindergasse in order to get into the Sarn Valley. But there was nobody there apart from some workers who were enjoying a glass of wine. I wondered what I should do. I did not want to spend the night in Bolzano. I was hungry and even more thirsty, but could not buy myself anything as I had no money and did not dare to beg. I left the inn feeling a little down-hearted. I was tired, and in addition my sore feet were painful. I decided to walk as far as I could and then to sleep in the grass at the side of the road.

When I set off it was shortly before nine o'clock and it was beginning to get dark. Above the "Deutschhaus" there was a wooden stick lying at the side of the road, which I took with me to use as a walking stick. I was not quite sure then whether I had found the right road to the Sarn Valley. But when I passed "Gschlößl-Stall" I knew that it was the right way. I trudged happily on in order to get home soon. The thought of home made me forget my tiredness and hunger a little. Meanwhile it had become dark and I came to the first tunnel. It was pitch-dark in the longer tunnels, just like being in a sack. I felt my way with my stick along the rock face until I was in the open air again. I was pleased when I had put the tunnels behind me. I was overcome by tiredness and tormented by thirst. I knew that in "Halbweg" there was a well beside the road. I wanted to quench my thirst there and was hoping to walk on more easily afterwards. It started to rain a little and I walked on along the road, half-asleep. There was nothing to disturb me, no cars or motorcycles, not even a human being.

Finally I came to "Halbweg" and heard the rushing of the water in the well. It was so dark that I could hardly recognize the trough. When I wanted to hold the food tin which I still carried with me under the stream of water, a big dog jumped out from behind the well and barked at me frighteningly. In that moment tiredness and thirst gave way to fright so that I quickly moved on.

It began to rain more heavily.

Severe tiredness set in again and I sat down repeatedly on the border stones at the side of the road and sometimes dropped off a little, until I almost fell off and got up in a fright to move on. After several rest breaks I came to Buntschen. Because it was raining heavily I wanted to find shelter for a short time somehow. I went to the small chapel and lent against the door. After I had said the Lord's Prayer several times, I was overcome by such great tiredness that I could no longer continue walking. I had to look for a shelter somewhere and went to Bundschen-Stadel, the door of which stood open. On the threshing floor there was a little grass and so I lay down on it and fell asleep immediately. I had been walking for four to five hours by this time.

I woke up when the bells were ringing to summon people to prayer. I went to the well and washed myself a little. It was probably around six o'clock. It had stopped raining, so I could go on. It was Sunday, the 19th of August, and

I met several people who were going home from the early mass. They were wearing their traditional Sunday costumes. I trudged on and finally arrived in Sarnthein. There I went immediately to Tutzer, a shop where my sister Anna lived with the owners. It was customary for relatives or acquaintances to leave their rucksack or shopping bags in the kitchen in order to be able to go shopping after the service.

At Tutzer I immediately met three of my siblings: Nanni, Burgl and Flor. The owners of the shop, Seppl and Gedl, were also there. It was a lovely surprise for all of us. I asked immediately about my four brothers who had been in the war. They were able to tell me with joy that all of them had finally returned home and that I was the last one.

Then my sister Moidl came in through the door. She hugged me and kissed me with joy.

In the meantime people had learnt what Dachau was and that for many it meant death. For that reason my relatives were afraid that I might not have survived it. They gave me a proper breakfast and then it was time to go to mass. In church I thanked the Lord God for my return home.

Afterwards I met three of my brothers. We told each other what we had been through and how we had got back home.

After the midday meal Flor and Burgl went with me to Reinswald to my parents. At that time you had to walk and I had to pull myself together in order to keep up. My siblings made me stop from time to time because they noticed that it was hard for me. I was limping more and more, my feet were painful because I had after all walked such a long distance the previous night. Whenever we came to a well, I had to drink a little. This had become a habit, and I thought that the fresh and clear spring water from the Sarn Valley would restore me.

And so we slowly approached my family home. When we left the main road to Durnholz and continued on the road to Reinswald, I saw a man coming towards us, wearing his Sunday costume. I recognized him right away: He was one of those responsible who had promised me and my parents that nothing would happen to me because I was a conscientious objector, but who had instead got me sentenced and taken to the concentration camp in Dachau. This gave me the shivers and I was overwhelmed by the fear which I had always had in the past of men like this. I would really have preferred to have got out of his way, but then I remembered that the tide had turned. Something like fighting spirit rose up within me: now I would defend myself. My brother Flor, who had also fled and narrowly escaped being caught by the then police officer and his local helpers, was not exactly pleased either to meet this man now.

When we came nearer he went up to me smiling, in his usual way, and offered to shake my hand by way of greeting, to which I responded, After he had said "Franz, hello, how are you?" he immediately turned to my siblings and said: "Now you can no longer threaten me with retaliation." That was what they had threatened him with were I to perish in Dachau. I think for him my homecoming was a relief, but on the other hand I remained a thorn in his flesh. We then went our own ways. But the joy of my homecoming was diminished by this encounter. This may have been for me the first rehearsal in forgiving, which I had repeatedly promised to do in the times of my greatest misery.

When we got home, only a younger sister and my youngest brother were there. My father worked as a herdsman on the alpine pasture, and my mother was at the Sunday afternoon service. I washed and changed my clothes because on the way home there had hardly been any opportunity to keep myself clean. It was a joy to put on civilian clothes. In the meantime my mother had come home and she was delighted that I had finally returned. She said that thank God the last of the six who had joined up or who had fled had also come home. Then she prepared us a modest snack. After a while I was sufficiently rested and felt strong enough to go to Durnholz, where I felt at home and where my boyhood friends lived.

At the Außerwegmann house I met my cousin Sanni in the evening, with whom I had grown up. She went with me to the Wegmann house where people were having their evening meal. Everybody was surprised at my arrival and invited me to join them in the meal because it was the Durnholz church festival. I accepted gladly. Other guests were there for the festival as well. One of them was "Klapf Flor", a relative of mine, who took an immediate interest in my experiences in Dachau, asked various questions and already knew that the concentration camp was supposed to be turned into a memorial and pilgrimage site.

After a while I went on because I really wanted to reach the Bachmann house, to see my foster-mother whom I loved very much. She had taken care of me as if I had been one of her own children so that we turned out to become worthwhile human beings. For that I am eternally grateful to her and to my dear foster-father, who died all too soon.

I went past the church and then walked along the lake. It was dark but in the dusk I could still make out the place where I had grown up. I saw the lights of the individual houses, and the path which I had taken hundreds of times to go to school and to church. I especially remember how I had always walked around in the darkness when I was on the run. I also remembered the old fisher folk from whom we boys from Hintersee had often borrowed the little boat to row around on the lake. In the front room of the little Schneider house a small lamp was still flickering. The well from which I had often had a drink, babbled beside the path and I felt more and more at home. I then saw the mother of the Schneider family going to the cow shed with a lantern. But she had not noticed me in the darkness. I trudged on, and on the way to Seeberhof I met my best school friend, Josef Hochkofler, nicknamed "Ebn-Sepp". We greeted one another and were both happy to have arrived home safely. He wanted me to go with him to Seeberhof where there was music and dancing. But I did not want to, and went on.

But Sepp told the people at Seeber's that I had come home and was on my way to Bachmann. My cousin and foster-brother, the Bachmann farmer Nikolaus Brugger, also heard this, came out of the house and shouted: "Franz, is that you?" I immediately recognized his voice and answered. I was already further up, above the farmhouse. So he told me to wait till he had caught up with me. I sat down at the side of the path on a stone, but I was eager to go on to reach the final destination of my homecoming.

We passed the Angerer farm, from where I had joined up, and came nearer and nearer to our destination. Soon I saw the house. Everything was dark in the house; the mother of the house was already in bed.

The farmer switched on the light, woke up my foster-mother, and we went into the living room to wait for her. We had hardly sat down when she came down from her room. She only wore a smock as she usually did when she was woken up at night. I can still remember her as she came in through the door, holding her smock together with one hand and extending the other hand towards me by way of greeting. She was happy about my homecoming and a few tears probably ran down my face.

I was at home.

After the meal which my foster-mother prepared, we chatted for a while until I was overcome by sleep. They told me where I could sleep and that I should have a rest. They gave me the room in which I had slept for fifteen years. Every knot-hole, every gap in the wall or in the floor was familiar to me, the murmuring of the water in the well in front of the house which was so nice to hear – all this added to my feeling of being at home. I probably said a prayer of thanks before I fell asleep.

And so the day of my homecoming, on which I had experienced so much of the joy of being reunited with my family, came to an end. I did not sleep as well as I had imagined and had all sorts of dreams. The day had been simply overwhelming.

In the morning I heard someone who was mowing the grass near the house for the cows sharpening his scythe. I also heard the cow bells which were so familiar to me and I could even imagine which cow was wearing which bell.

I stayed in bed because they had suggested I should do so, and it was pleasant to sleep in a bed again after such a long time.

I thought about what might happen now. I did not want to be a burden to anybody, but I was still too weak to work. I got up and had breakfast, which the young farmer's wife prepared for me. I thanked her for everything and went to the neighbour, Angerer, where I had my wardrobe, because in the previous year I had been employed there as a farm hand and it was from there that I had joined up. I took a few items of clothes out of my wardrobe and the farmer's wife then also gave me something to eat. She was alone at home and asked if I wanted to stay. They could do with my help as there was a lot of work to be done at that time. Her suggestion caused me some embarrassment because I felt I owed something for everything which I had received when I was on the run and for the food which I had been allowed to take with me, but my physical condition did not make it possible for me to work yet. I said I would have to recover a little first. She understood that and said that I should come as soon as I could.

A New Beginning

After that I went home to my mother and I thought about what I should do in the future. My brother Pius was staying with our mother in Unterreinswald and had his workshop in the basement in which I too had worked in the winter of 1941/42. We had made buttons and cigarette lighters and I had learned how to engrave from him. My brother would have employed me as an assistant. I quite liked working with metal, but I had the impression that I had not yet found my vocation.

The following day I went with my mother to Sarnthein to register at the town hall and pick up my food stamps. I handed over my provisional discharge document to the town official. He looked at it and read it for a while, then turned to me and said I would have to go to the discharge camp in Bolzano in order to be discharged from there, because he could not register me otherwise and give me any food stamps.

I collapsed inwardly. I was supposed to go into a prison camp once again although I had only been discharged from such a camp a few days before?

No, never again would I set foot in a camp and certainly not voluntarily, whatever might happen. I felt dispensable and thought that I should not have come home. I became furious and said, almost in tears: "I have had enough of camps!" First of all I had been tortured almost to death in the concentration camp by starvation, disease and hard labour; afterwards I endured all sorts of agonies as a prisoner of the Americans, and now I am supposed to go into a camp once again! All this did not seem to make the official give me any food stamps. I wanted to leave and said that I certainly would not starve to death. Then my mother started pleading with him and he gave me the stamps.

We went to the Tutzer grocery shop to buy a few small items. The sparse income of my mother and the five hundred lire which my sister had given me did not go far. On the way home I met a relative, Josef Thaler, nicknamed "Ebner Sepp" who, together with my former school friend, Jakob Ainhäuser, nicknamed "Kofler Joggele", was a cowherd on the mountain pastures at Seeb. Both of them had already heard on Sunday that I had come home. I was given Joggele's message to come to join him on the mountain pastures in order to have a rest, and I gladly accepted the invitation.

I set off straight away on the following day. We had a very great deal to tell one other. Sepp had joined up in 1942, had fought on the Russian front and had been wounded quite a few times. After his furlough in spring 1944 he had not returned but fled to the mountains. In the winter he had stayed in a barn which had hay and had waited in the mountains for the end of the war to come. Joggel had also been on the run. All three of us had suffered great misery which we had the whole Nazi system and, last but not least, the local people to thank for.

I had an enjoyable time in the mountains until Saturday.

That Sunday was the Reinswald church festival. I met many friends and acquaintances from near and far, and also some who did not want to meet me. I made no difference between them and greeted them all, but I noticed immediately that those who had been enthusiastic supporters of Hitler avoided talking to me. I was very sensitive in this matter then, felt an inner aversion against these people, but did not let them notice anything. The church festival went on as usual with joy and merriment.

That Monday I went to Angerer in Durnholz in order to work off my debts from the previous year. The farmers used to say that the week of the church festival in the Sarn Valley was the hardest week of the whole year. The work was difficult for me, all my limbs hurt, and my hands were covered with blisters. Work on the steep hills was particularly difficult. I was glad when the week was over and kept thinking secretly about lighter work. On Monday I went to the church festival market where I met my brother Pius. He again offered me work and I immediately accepted it, because in my condition I was up to this kind of work but not to farm work. A week later I picked up the chest with my clothes from Angerer. The farm people were a little annoyed at first because I did not stay with them. A farmhand mentioned that I did not want to work any more. At that time only farm work counted for many people.

I felt comfortable in my brother's workshop.

About three weeks later I received a letter from the council. I would have to pick up a parcel which had been sent to every prisoner of a concentration camp by the state. I went right away the following day and the official was obviously surprised to see me so soon. He thought for a while and then took me into the next room. What did I see there? The parcel had been torn open and the clothes were lying spread out on the floor. He said I should pack everything up and I put everything in my rucksack. There was a pair of pants, a vest, a shirt, a pair of trousers and a jacket. I was pleased about the clothes because I needed them badly. I had really only the bare necessities. Some of my clothes had been left behind in Dachau, others had become too small for me. I had only a pair of two differently sized shoes from my time as a prisoner. From a blanket which my sister had given me my mother sewed a pair of trousers as Sunday best, and my brother Flor gave me a jacket. I was that poor at the time.

When I unpacked my clothes parcel at home I saw that the official had exchanged my new jacket for his old patched up one. This no longer went with the trousers and had sleeves which were too short for me, but just the right length for this small official. I was furious with this man. He was obviously the sort of person who had sent me to the concentration camp and who was capable of doing anything, however bad. I lost all my trust in officialdom, became suspicious of all of them. Would it have been better I had not come home at all? I was in any case afraid of everything that had to do with authority, and particularly with the police and the military. It took me years to overcome this fear.

First of all I had to try to assert myself and not be a burden to anyone. I made so much money at my brother's that

I was slowly able to buy the necessary clothes and to contribute to the food at home.

In 1946 I went to my brother Johann in Sarnthein to learn quill embroidery. I worked there for about two months. At that time there was no legally binding period of apprenticeship for this profession. After my brother had taught me the most important things I started to work independently and had to learn various things by myself. I worked with enthusiasm and often sat at my work for twelve to fourteen hours at a time. There was no shortage of orders as this profession was almost dying out.

My brother and I certainly had a lot of work but there was no question of becoming rich. People after the war had no money, particulary a poor farmhand who – as was the custom at that time – received his small payment only once a year. So we often had to wait for a long time to receive the pay which we had honestly earned.

I made more and more good friends who helped me overcome all my problems so that after the hard experiences I was able to experience some happy years as a young man with them.

Shortly after the war I joined up with several repatriates to discuss erecting a war memorial. As a repatriate I felt obliged to the victims of the war to do something for them, to put up a memorial for them. Others too, who had been persecuted by the Nazis, had the same idea. We invited the builder, Josef Thaler, Häusler, to advise us and to make a design. He too had been arrested by the Nazis because of his sympathy for those who were "anti-Hitler" and had spent some time in various prisons. We had a marble plate inscribed with the names of the fallen and missing from our village, and I was happy to help with the ensuing work. Then came the festive consecration of the war memorial, at which both the young and old in our community enjoyed themselves. This made it easier to remember the victims of the war and to pray for them.

I probably never missed an opportunity before or after the service to stand in front of the war memorial in order to pray for the victims of the war.

We homecomers also took care of the memorial and organized a memorial service every year which the then priest, Alois Vigl, managed to lead in a particularly solemn way. In his reflective and moving addresses many an eye welled up with tears, particulary among the homecomers who themselves had often narrowly escaped death, but also among many relatives of the war victims.

A few years later the memorial service was changed a little. The war victims were now made into war heroes. But who performed heroic deeds for Hitler? Only those who had fallen victim to the fraudulent propaganda could become war heroes. The others were forced to fight under threat of being shot or – what was even worse – of being sent to a concentration camp. They were all war victims.

Foreign "heroes" were also invited and then we "war traitors" or "war criminals", as we were called, had no longer a part to play. Only the very brave who had fought loyally for the Führer until the end, were allowed to step in front of the war memorial as heroes. During the ceremony we stood somewhere among the people and prayed for our comrades because nobody could after all forbid us to do that. After the church service they told people about their heroic deeds and whoever listened carefully could catch many a hymn of praise for Hitler. The war victims sometimes seemed only to be an excuse; in reality they were celebrating themselves.

Now, forty years after the war, it is left only to us to remember the war victims and we do so as we did at the beginning.

Twenty years after the liberation from the concentration camp of Dachau I decided to visit this memorial place into which it had been transformed, and view this place of horror and fear in peace and quiet. I went to Munich by train and from there on to Dachau. The camp was already closed as it was after five p.m. I wanted to look for a place to stay for the night. As it was raining very heavily I did not want to walk around for long and went into a bar near the camp. I asked the waitress whether there was a guesthouse somewhere nearby where I could spend the night. She said there was none, and said that I would have to go into the town of Dachau.

Meanwhile some young lads who were sitting in the bar had noticed me and wanted to tease me. They said that I could sleep at the waitress's place. I was annoyed and said to them: "That's how you Germans are! First you almost tortured me to death in the concentration camp and now I am supposed to let myself be teased by you!" One of the lads got up, apologized and said it had only been a joke, I should calm down and if I agreed he would drive me into town. I asked him to do that and in a short time he found me accommodation in a guesthouse in town. I wanted to pay him

172

but he did not accept anything. So I thanked him and went to my night's lodgings.

Although everything was alright I did not go to sleep that evening for a long time. All sorts of thoughts went through my head; I remembered everything I had seen and experienced in the camp.

In the morning, after breakfast, I attended holy mass in a nearby church. Afterwards I went back to the guesthouse and was able to drive immediately to the camp with the landlord.

I learned that on that day the Protestant church was to be ceremoniously inaugurated. I went into the camp; everything seemed strange to me, even the entrance which was now situated on the opposite side of the former main gate. The barracks had all been torn down except for two of them. Only the office building, the Jourhaus*, below which the gate with the motto "Arbeit macht frei" was situated and the bunker on the right of the entrance, behind the administrative building, remained. I joined the other visitors and took part in the inauguration ceremony which was organized by the Protestants and Catholics together. There were a lot of important clerical and secular people there. They prayed and sang together and during the addresses many broke down in tears.

Two years after this I went back to Dachau on the day of liberation, the 29th of April. This time I arrived in the camp at midday and decided to have a thorough look at every-

---

* Translators' footnote: The entrance building controlled by the SS and through which all prisoners had to pass

173

thing. I did not look at my watch and overran the opening time by half an hour. As I was busy taking photographs of the memorial plaques behind the trees and bushes, the camp attendants had not seen me. While I was standing there and thinking, somebody spoke to me and asked me what I was doing there. It was a woman who, with her husband, was responsible for keeping the camp tidy and who also lived there. I explained to her what I had experienced and suggested that she could let me out. She said that this was not possible because she did not have a key for the gate, and her husband, who had the key, was nowhere to be found at that time. Her husband said that they would have to telephone the police, but his wife invited me to spend the night on a bench in a side room in their flat.

I could not get to sleep for a while. All sorts of thoughts were going through my mind. I was in fact in the crematorium building. I could remember well the smoke from the crematorium which, depending on the direction of the wind, drifted through the camp, and the stench of burnt bones. We could always tell whether it was the new arrivals who still had fat on their body who were being burnt. In this case blackish yellow smoke ascended. But in the case of the others, who had been in the camp longer, and were only skin and bone, the smoke which ascended was thin and blue.

After that night I returned home satisfied. I had refreshed my memories a bit, but rarely spoke about them, and only when somebody asked. Most of those who had been in the war had much more to say than I did. This is when I always used to withdraw and kept everything to myself, almost like a secret.

After this I went to Dachau several times, also with my daughters, and later, thirty-five years after liberation once again with the whole family.

Frequently I was asked by various organizations to accompany them on trips to Dachau. It would be very impressive if somebody were with them who himself had experienced Dachau and could talk about his own experiences.

This is how the young people of Reinswald organized, in 1985 – forty years after the liberation from National Socialism – two trips to Dachau, to one of which I invited the historian, Leopold Steurer, and Erich Pichler who had shared my suffering.

Also trips to Dachau were organized from other parts of the country: Kaltern, Eppan, Neumarkt, Latzfons, Klausen, Brixen ... And always it was the young who initiated them. It was always a joy for me to go with them. I even felt obliged to show them what National Socialism had led to. Many South Tyrolians had become its victims, whether voluntarily or under coercion. I am particulary pleased that young people are interested in this chapter of history. They have the right to learn the truth about this era, which has been kept secret from them for over forty years and which – so it seems to me – people would still like to keep secret.

Afterword

If this book can make a small contribution to the education of those who know little about that time and to make the fantical supporters of Hitler aware that not everything has been forgotten, then it has fulfilled its purpose. It is not intended to be an indictment of those who had done wrongs against some of those who had voted to remain Italian citizens, one might even say those who thought differently. I for my part have forgiven them.

I know that someone who writes about the Hitler era as I do will be branded an outsider and put down as a grumbler. But I also know who I am and I trust myself to tell the truth about that time. I have never harmed anyone; I simply did not agree to fight for the Nazi regime in foreign countries, and as an Italian citizen I did not feel obliged to do so.

Nowadays some say one should not draw attention to past atrocities. But I say: everyone should learn the whole truth about that time and learn from it so that it is not repeated. Some would like to to cover up the bad things then with present evils. They are unlikely to succeed in doing so, except perhaps with those young people who themselves are not interested because in schools this period of history is still, to a certain extent, suppressed.

Whenever somebody asked me about my experiences in Dachau I was often interrupted in my description by those who had a different opinion and who then said that it was finally time to stop talking about these old matters and to forgive and forget. I could only always say the same thing to them: "You have no idea about everything there is to be forgotten and forgiven." People cannot imagine the physical and mental torture in the concentration camps unless they have experienced it themselves. I think that we who were persecuted by the Nazis were generous in our forgiving. The Nazis heard nothing from us apart from a few swear words. In the worst case someone had to take a cool "bath" in a well or was slapped in the face.

The Nazis were repeatedly given the opportunity for reconciliation but their old Nazi pride did not permit them to own up to a single one of their old mistakes. It is easy to forgive someone when he admits his mistakes. It is more difficult if somebody denies all guilt, even if his guilt can be proven.

I have never heard anyone say he should not have done or said something – neither the simplest "voter for Germany" who mocked us as "Walsche", nor the big village Nazis who unjustly sent me and others to the concentration camp or to prison or to the front. On the contrary, quite a few secret Nazi spies who were nevertheless well-known in public to every-one, stated again and again that they had not been involved and had not betrayed anyone. Or very often you could hear the great excuse: "We had to do it, otherwise we would have had to join up immediately." So they stayed at home at the expense of others whom they unscrupulously imprisoned.

There is one thing I still have not understood even now: why they mocked and persecuted us as "Walsche". No one has so far wanted or dared to give an answer to this question.

But everything was, after all, forgiven.

So I also received orders for quill embroidery from those who I had reason to suspect had sent me to the concentration camp. I was pleased to be needed by them now, although they would have preferred to "eradicate" me at that time. If the dear Lord is merciful to them as well, which I would wish for them, then everything is alright.

With regard to forgetting, that is more difficult. I have forgiven but not forgotten. And I make an effort not to forget. In the museum at Dachau you can read the words: "Whoever does not remember the past is condemned to go through it again."

This little book is supposed to help a little to prevent this from happening.

Even Reinhold Messner rekindled memories of the past with his exaggerated statement that ninety percent of the South Tyrolians had betrayed their homeland at the time of option. But he was not completely wrong because I must say a large percentage had followed the true traitors and made a mockery of us.

The book by Friedl Volgger also brought some life into the discussion of the history of that time, and although he, as it seemed to me, treated his opponents very gently, he was attacked by many.

Some people could not stand the trips to Dachau at all, although they were always organized as reflective trips (a memorial trip, a peace trip, a penitence trip ...).

People no longer want to hear about the faults of the Germans. Are they ashamed of what they did to us? Why not? It is no disgrace to feel shame for wrongs which have been committed. A German guest, a longstanding friend of mine, once asked me why I could be so friendly and nice to the Germans, since I had after all suffered so much at their hands. I can be friendly to everyone as long as people do not offend me.

The political development in South Tyrol fills me with some anxiety.

After the war people were suspicious. They thought that the people's party was another party like the Nazi party before it, and did not want to be taken in again by such a scam. But the founders of the people's party were those who promoted what was "German", but this time it was what was "Tyrolian German", and they defended their position. Those who had the other sense of "German" in mind crept in again and wanted to have their voice heard. This was certainly a reason to be suspicious. The situation was particularly tense in the sixties. I will never approve of the bomb attacks of those years, even if we hear from various quarters nowadays that they were necessary. I sometimes became annoyed when I walked through the city of Bolzano at that time and came across Italians who regarded me as a dangerous terrorist. I could not blame them for this because I, as always, was wearing the traditional dress of the Sarn Valley. But many Italians believed that everyone who wore traditional costume was a gunman, and as such a terrorist. I explained this to quite a few Italians and said that those who were not ashamed to go to

Bolzano wearing traditional costume were the most harmless ones.

Another event which caused only bad feeling and destroyed a lot of trust was the so-called "Crown of Thorns" which was carried through Innsbruck in 1984. A farmer with a sense of humour once made a fitting remark to somebody who had taken part enthusiastically: "In Innsbruck you carried the crown of thorns, and we now have to carry the cross."

In the fanatic German traditionalists there is a good portion of the Hitler mentality which is kept alive by the old Nazis, who still have not come to terms with their defeat. I do not think, and do not hope, that people become enthusiastic about the Neonazis in Germany and follow them, although throughout South Tyrol there are such people, even among the politicians, who do not really object to the rising National Socialism abroad.

I would like to say to our young people: remain South Tyrolians but be tolerant towards those who speak another language and with whom we live. Keep away those who do to you what they did to us.

The question of heroism has preoccupied me since the time when I was regarded as inferior or as a traitor by many fighters on the front. Many of those who voted to stay Italian citizens thought that after the occupation of South Tyrol by the Germans in 1943 that it would not last long until the war was over and that they would pull through with the help of a few good friends, and fled. I think that required more courage than marching along with the crowd. They wanted, if it really came to it, to give up their lives at home rather than in a foreign country where they were actually not fighting for their homeland.

It took no less courage to hand oneself over to the authorities, to face uncertainty and to experience the suffering of the concentration camp. Every soldier on the front – had he come into the concentration camp – would have immediately left to go back to the front because there he was somehow still a human being and could defend himself. However, in the concentration camp one was at the mercy of the whims of the SS. The terror which was created in the concentration camp was ten times as great as the fear on the front. As someone put it, the experience of a single prisoner was sufficient to keep ten soldiers on the front.

For me heroes are those people who save human lives, even at the risk of losing their own lives. Heroes were those who dared to stand up against the lies of Hitler's propaganda and defended their own beliefs. Heroes are also those who, after the war, took a stand for a German South Tyrol and reintegrated even those who had denied themselves the right to be South Tyrolians.

I cannot conclude without my sincere thanks to those who helped me through the time which I have described. Those are the people from whom, in the spring and summer of 1944, I received food and lodging during the nights, or who gave me provisions. Many people helped me by warning me of dangers and not betraying me, although it would have been their "strict duty" to have done so. They knew what could have happened to them if they had been found out. Probably Christian humanity meant more to them than dubious regulations. I would also like to thank those who helped my two brothers who had fled in the final months of the war and all the other resistance fighters by providing food and lodging, and who saved them from many dangers. All of them together played their part in saving human lives and bringing the war to a swifter conclusion. I owe my greatest thanks to those who helped me in the concentration camp and imprisonment and who sometimes saved me from certain death. I would also like to thank those who fortunately did not know about all of our suffering but kept praying for us. I say again and again: a strong belief in God and prayer have helped me overcome many hardships and contributed to my final homecoming. I have never forgotten to thank the Lord God and the Mother of God.

Finally I would like to thank those who now have the courage, and spare no pains, to stand up for peace, particularly the women and young people, but also the men. I wish them the strength to achieve their goals so that more and more people come to understand that life in peace and modesty, in love and support for your neighbour, can be good.

Franz Thaler
Reinswald, 1988

Franz Thaler

Franz Thaler was born in Reinswald in South Tyrol on 6 March 1925.

In the referendum ("Option") in 1939 his father decided that the whole family should remain Italian citizens. Despite this Thaler was called up to do military service in the German Wehrmacht in 1944 at the age of 19. Instead of enlisting he fled to the mountains, but gave himself up when his family was threatened with reprisals. He was arrested and sent to Dachau where he spent about five months. When the Americans arrived in Dachau he became a prisoner-of-war of the Americans and was taken to a camp in France, where he was finally set free and allowed to return home. After the war he became a craftsman in quill embroidery, and continued to work until his recent retirement. After publishing his memoir of Dachau in 1988 ("Unvergessen", now available in Raetia Verlag, Bolzano), he did educational work with young people, which included accompanying them on trips to Dachau. In 1997 he received the Verdienstkreuz des Landes Tirol (Order of Merit of the Land of Tyrol) and in 2010 he was awarded the honorary citizenship of Bolzano. In 2012 he was honoured as Political Personality of the Year by the South Tyrolean Society of Political Sciences in Bozen. An opera based on his memoir of Dachau, *Unforgotten – the Opera*, has been composed by Enguerrand-Friedrich Lühl (musical director Richard Sigmund) and performed in the Walther-Haus/Bozen in 2004 (look for "Thaler Unvergessen" in YouTube; the first three results on this page are links to the three acts of the opera).

Franz Thaler died on 29 October 2015 in Sarnthein, South Tyrol.